Path to Eternal Truth

Volume ll

Manjula Rao

BALBOA.
PRESS
A DIVISION OF HAY HOUSE

Balboa Press books may be ordered through booksellers or by contacting:

Balboa Press
A Division of Hay House
1663 Liberty Drive
Bloomington, IN 47403
www.balboapress.com.au
1 (877) 407-4847

Print information available on the last page.

ISBN: 978-1-5043-1405-3 (sc)
ISBN: 978-1-5043-1404-6 (e)

Balboa Press rev. date: 07/30/2018

Acknowledgements

When passion rules our senses, it leads to downfall. However, this same passion is required to strengthen our principles. A devotee should staunchly stand by his or her principles. I would like to thank all the divine souls who helped me on this wonderful, memorable spiritual journey.

Thank you to my guru, His Holiness Jagadguru Shankaracharya Swami Swaroopananda Sarasvati, who has been my guiding force and whose presence I feel every moment in my life.

Thank you to my family members, who supported me in my work—my husband, Sudhindra Rao; my daughters Priyanka and Pooja, my son-in-law Anuraag, my sister Sharmila, my mother Savitri as my first Guru, and my father Murugesan, who was my role model and taught me the lessons of life.

An additional thank you to all my team in Luxmy Furniture, Sydney, Australia.

About My Guru

Gurudev preaches Love, Joy, Abundance and Happiness which can be achieved by following the path of Righteousness. SANATANA DHARMA the eternal law, is about living a fulfilling and more invigorating lifestyle.

Pujya Gurudev is the present SHANKARACHARYA OF DWARAKA in the West and Jyotishpeeth in the North of India.

Gurudev had two sisters Kusum and Geeta and four brothers who were Ramnath, Ramraksha, Hargovind and Ahivaran.

He was called Pothiram as he was always interested in reading the scriptures. As a child Pothi used to sit and read scriptures when his brothers used to play. Pothi left the house at the age of thirteen and studied till then in Dighori which was his birth place.

He met Swami Shivanand in the year 1938 and Swamiji had a great impact on Pothi. Swamiji predicted that Pandit Dhanpati Upadhyay and Shrimati Girija Upadhyay will have a son who will be a great saint one day whose name and fame will spread in the entire universe. Both his parents were pious, religious, loving, and very caring. Pothi used to listen to the Bhagavad Geeta, Ramayana from his parents and he would then go and relate the stories to his neighbours. This became a habit and very soon he became a well versed "KATHA VACHAK" one who can relate from the scriptures and in this way he used to revise the scriptures he heard from his parents.

Dhanpath Upadhyay died when Pothi was very young. He did not shed a tear and this worried his mother. He used to sit under a Neem tree and contemplate on Birth and Death. He would say mother why are you crying? Father has gone to heaven where you too will go and so will my brothers and sisters and later on I too will join all of you. Gurudev also said "You should not have the Desire to Live or the Desire to die".

Gurudev's Discourses are DIVINE and listening to them takes you to another planet straight away. He relates every Shloka from the Bhagavad Geeta with a story that has a moral. His Shishyas are spell bound and not one of them wants to leave the place where Gurudev has his discourse. He makes every shishya feel very special and thus the bond between the Guru and the Shishya becomes stronger. He has till now initiated more than 5oo million Shishyas. His Shishyas come from all over the world. Gurudev indeed is the incarnation of ADI GURU SHANKARACHARYA.

Gurudev discovered the cave in which GURU GOVINDPADACHARYA gave Danda Diksha to Shankara who then became Adi Guru Shankaracharya. Govind Vanam is in Sakal Ghat on the banks of the river Narmada.

Pothi met Dandi Swami Muktanand Sarasvati ji, at the age of fourteen. He wanted to study further so he left for Mughwani with his brother Ramraksha who joined the police force. He met Swami Muktanand in Mughwani when Swamiji came to Mughwani for Chaturmaas. Pothi was very happy as he could now go for satsangh and hear swamiji's pravachan, everyday for two months. He wanted his mother to come for Chaturmaas. Ramraksha advised him to write a letter inviting his mother for chaturmaas. Ramraksha the elder brother of Pothi took Danda Diksha from him and now at the ripe age of 96 he lives in Varanasi. Both the brothers have the same loving look and have a great sense of HUMOUR which is hard to find among Sanyasis of such a high order.

Pothi studied for five years in a Sanskrit Pathshala in Narsinghpur. Later he studied in Rampur Sanskrit Pathshala, Ichval gram, Ghazipur Zilla, U P, for two years under Bhola Singh who was his teacher, who soon became very attached and fond of Pothi, for whom he built a house which he named as "Mukti Kutir".

In the year 1942 he met Hariharanand later known as Karapartri ji. Both of them spent a lot of time together. Pothiram and Hariharanand observed Chaturmaas from 1942 in Varanasi for fourteen years at "Karapartri Dham" Dharm Sangh.

Karapartriji got Gurudev to take Diksha for Danda Sanyasa from Shankaracharya Swami Brahmananda Sarasvati ji of Jyothirmath in Calcutta at Lekhram Kothi, on 31st December 1949.

Gurudev took Shri Vidya Diksha from Karapartriji. Later Gurudev learnt "KUNDALINI YOGA" from Pritam Das, Phulwari Ashram, Jhalon Zilla, U P.

In 1942 he was once again imprisoned for cutting the telephone lines of the British Government. The British Officials were quite afraid of Gurudev as he was a very Fierce Young Dynamic Sanyasi.

Gurudev did Bhagavad on the banks of the Bain Ganga River.

Gurudev was a young revolutionary MONK, Sanyasi, As a Freedom Fighter at the age of 26 he was jailed in Varanasi for 9 months.

Guruji achieved his SIDDHI POWERS from "BRAHMA KUND" which is on the banks of the River Narmada close to Sakal Ghat.

After achieving SIDDHI POWERS he wanted a serene, quite, place nestled in the lap of nature to do his SADHANA and TAPASYA. He soon found "VICHAR SHILA" with all the wild animals and having found all that he was looking for he did his Tapasya for 12 continuous long years and achieved "REALISATION".

Pothi met Hariharanand (Karpartriji) in 1942.

On 7th December 1973 at, Shankaracharya Bhavan, Krishna Bodhashram, Kothi No 7, New Delhi. Gurudev was annointed as the Shankaracharya of JYOTHIRMATH.

Gurudev's ABHISHEK was done by Swami Hariharanand Sarasvatiji (Karapartriji) Shankaracharya Swami Niranjandev Tirth and Dwaraka Sharadha peeth Shankaracharya Swami Abhinav Sachidanand Tirth, Representatives of Shankaracharya Of Sringeri Sharadha Peeth, Chala Laxman Shastri and Vasant Gargil. Central Minister Chaudhary Neetraj Singh.

On 27th May 1982 at Dwaraka, Gurudev was annointed as the Shankaracharya of Dwaraka Sharadha Peeth. In the Shankaracharya Parampara after Adi Guru Shankaracharya, Gurudev is the only Dandi Sanyasi to be annointed as Shankaracharya of two seats. He was chosen by Shankaracharya Swami Abhinav Sachidanand Tirth of Dwaraka, as it was written in his will that after he leaves the physical body Gurudev should be the next Shankaracharya of Dwaraka as he is qualified, educated, experienced, and the incarnation of Adi Guru Shankaracharya. For the ABHISHEK Shankaracharya Swami Abhinav Vidya Tirth, and his shishya Bharti Tirth, the present Shankaracharya of Sringeri were present along with the minister of Gujarat.

Tolaram Nema a resident of Shridham was present at this auspicious occasion and he carried Gurudev's Padukas.

On 27th May 1982, Gurudev was annointed as the Shankaracharya of Dwaraka. In the Shankaracharya Parampara Gurudev is the only Dandi Sanyasi who occupies two seats.

It is rare to see a sanyasi so caring, who has studied the scriptures, travelled the country and compassionate. He is also known as "Dharam Samrat" which means emperor of righteousness.

Gurudev always cares for the ADIVASIS. Every year Gurudev distributes clothes, food, medicines to them at Vishwa Kalyan Ashram in Jharkhand. He is a Saint who always thinks for the needy, handicapped, old and sick.

Gurudev was born on September 2nd in the year 1924, in a village called DIGHORI which is in the district of SIVANI. He came from a Brahmin family with a strict religious and spiritual background. His parents were loving and pious. His Father was Shri Dhanapati Upadhyaya and his mother was Shrimati Girija Devi who named him Pothiram. Pothi means Shastra which is our scriptures. He is said to be the incarnation of the Shastras. Born in a pious and spiritual family, his quest for truth was aroused at a young age of nine and soon he left on a pilgrimage. He went to Varanasi where he studied the Vedas which are the four pillars of HINDUISM. He further studied the Vedangas, Puranas, Smritis and the text on Nyaya from many divine souls.

At this time Gurudev participated in the Indian Independence Movement and in 1942 was jailed by the British Empire. At the age of 19 itself he created a name for himself by being known as a "Revolutionary Monk" and soon got involved in the struggle for freedom.

He was imprisoned twice and served a term of nine months in the Varanasi prison, and another term of six months in a Narsingpur prison in Madhya Pradesh.

In the year 1950 he was initiated into the rare and exalted order of "DAND SANYAS". As a Dandi Swami he followed the foot steps of Shri Adi Shankaracharya (Grand Sire of ADVAITA).

On the seventh of December in the year 1973 Gurudev was anointed as the SHANKARACHARYA OF JYOTISHPEETH. He took over the duties of Shankaracharya, spreading the message of compassion, love and humility among the people. His name soon spread far and wide and when the Shankaracharya of Dwaraka Sharadha Peeth left his physical body he requested Gurudev to take over the seat of Dwaraka, and he stated the same in his will. In the Shankaracharya Parampara, Gurudev is the only Shankaracharya who occupies two seats.

He is a liberated sage who has always followed 'SANATANA DHARMA' throughout his life. He is a living example of our scriptures. At the age of 93 he still works non stop and helps the indigenous tribes. He has helped in guiding the nation towards resolution of some vexing and emotional issues. One of them was concerning the RAM SETU BRIDGE between India and Sri Lanka. The bridge was to be demolished but it was only because of Gurudev that the demolition was stopped. The other major issue Gurudev helped resolve was the 60 year old dispute over the land where LORD SHRI RAM was born. Hindus and Muslims could not come to a mutually satisfying solution. GURUDEV guided them towards the peaceful solution of building a temple and a mosque on the same land by maintaining a distance between them. This, as GURUDEV says, prevents one being disturbed by the other. Thus the bells of the temple do not disturb their Muslim brothers who are doing their Namaz and the loud speakers from the Mosque do not disturb the Hindu families doing their prayers in the temple.

GURUDEV runs many VEDA pathshalas, Sanskrit schools and Ayurvedic dispensaries. He promotes the Spiritual Path to the entire Humanity by travelling all around North and West of India.

The sheer grace of Gurudev's presence is enough to wipe one's slate clean of all the worries, anxieties and psychosomatic ailments which cloud the path to 'Eternal Happiness'.

Advaita is a way of Life and it was first propounded by Sri Adi Shankaracharya who was born in the year 507 B.C. His Holiness in his book 'The Path to Eternal Truth' has given the principles of 'Sanantan Dharma' the Eternal Law which has no beginning and no end. By following his teachings one can bring in abundance into their life and spread love, joy, and Happiness.

Chapter 1

SEEK SHELTER IN GOD

Our *sastras* consider *dharma* (righteousness), *artha* (wealth), *kama* (desire), and *moksa* (liberation) to be the four goals. Man makes one, two or all of these his purpose and absorbs himself in attaining them through various means. As against this, some devotees relinquish the desire for these four goals and instead, totally devote themselves to the worship of God. According to them, the love for God is the fifth goal.

If one thinks it over, one realises that the main cause for all attainments is *dharma*. The attainment of *artha* and *kama* depends upon the *dharma* of one's present or past lives. The *jnana,* the means of attaining *moksa,* the awakening of devotion can take place only in the

1

mind that is free from desire and purified by following *dharma*. *Dharma* also forms the basis of making *dharma* the goal. In this modern age, people are forgetting this principle. This is because the basis of religious belief is the eternal nature of the soul and the power of the omnipresent, omniscient God. But Man today is forgetting this. If these two beliefs are firmly established in the heart of Man, he can never falter from the path of *dharma*. It is confirmed that after death, the individual soul persists as it has to bear the fruits of the good and bad *karma* performed in the present life. The omniscient God is aware of all of Man's *karma* and accordingly decides to bestow upon Man the life that he deserves, decides how long he should live and what are the experiences he has to go through. However as clever a person may be, nothing about him remains hidden from God, as "You can deceive those with two eyes but never the One with a thousand eyes".

> ***rama jharokha baithake sabaka mujara leya***
> ***jakÍ jaisÍ cakarÍ tako taiso deya.***
> -This excerpt has been taken from the teachings of Saint KabÍra.

God gives us the fruits of our *karma* and controls the entire universe. He is omniscient and insightful. Insightful is the one who lives in this world and has control over it. God shows the right path to those who have faltered from it. He favours *dharma*, *nyaya* and *sadguna*. He destroys arrogance and vanity in Man being beyond the universe. Unobtrusively, He discourages evil qualities and encourages divine ones. He is the sole support of the needy, weak and the distressed. If Man becomes blinded due to the intoxication of his wealth, youth and luxuries and becomes oblivious to God, there will come a day when God will create a situation which will compel Man to open his eyes and realise his mistake.

Sometimes God sends a warning to the mind which people call the inner voice. However, not everyone can hear it. It gets suppressed due to the predominance of desires. In fact, some people are deluded into thinking that their desires are the urging of God. Only can the person whose mind is free from desires, who has relinquished his wants, has surrendered himself to God, and considers himself to be a machine and God as the operator, can hear His voice.

Lord *Krsna* says in the *GÍta*

> **isvarah sarvabhutanam**
> **hrddeser'juna tisthati**
> **bhramayan sarvabhutani**

yantrarudhani mayaya
tam eva saranam gaccha
sarvabhavena bharata
tatprasadat param
santim sthanam prapsyasi sasvatam

- BhagavadgÍta 18. 61

"Oh *Arjuna* ! The insightful Supreme Being, mounted atop the machine which is Man, resides in his heart and in accordance to Man's *karma*, takes him on a journey with his supernatural powers".

"Oh *Bharata* ! Seek shelter in God. Only there, with His blessings, will you find true peace and a permanent refuge".

When the *mana* (mind), *vacana* (words) and *karma* (deeds) are all devoted to God, *adharma* cannot touch the person. He will never lie, never have evil thoughts and his senses will never go *astraya*. Only such a person is considered to be truly virtuous and benevolent towards others. The benevolence of a person who disregards the Lord, only feeds his own ego. However, those who have sought shelter in God (*saranagati*) have an egoless benevolence and have a simple nature.

para upakara vacana mana kaya
santa svabhava sahaja khagaraya

To be truly benevolent, one has to sacrifice selfishness. However, when the limited ego is present, all deeds of Man, knowingly or unknowingly, are for selfish purposes and for the satisfaction of the ego. It is impossible to be selfless in such a state. Those who have laid down their lives for their community, society and their country are called selfless. Actually, upon reflection, the boundaries of their selfishness widen, but the selfishness remains. The one who totally dedicates and surrenders himself to the Supreme Power or God, is the one who is truly selfless.

This Supreme Power which continuously pours out love and compassion is reflected through the *mana*, *vacana* and *karma* of those dedicated to Him.

Man today, is in search of peace. It is a rule that Man, for the fulfillment of his purpose, should adopt means which are in accordance with his philosophical beliefs. "Fulfillment of desires brings peace". This has become the philosophy of our lives today. However, this is wrong. Fulfillment of one desire gives rise to many more desires which, being impossible to fulfill, give rise to discontentment or restlessness. The one who is restless will never find peace. **"asantasya kutah sukham"** In other words, only can the elimination of desires bring peace and happiness but those who disregard God will never be free of desires and hence will never find true happiness. By renouncing worldly attachments and dedicating oneself to the one and only God and seeking shelter in His highest abode and through endless faith and devotion to him, can one turn towards God. This is the *saranagati*. Desire and selfishness are permanently eliminated from the heart of a *saranagata* devotee. The *Vedas* say that God has thousands of heads, thousands of limbs and thousands of eyes and in reality, our body, senses, mind and intellect are all parts of that vast, universal Supreme Being. We have mistakenly considered ourselves to be different from God. In fact, all that we have belongs to him. What is there for us to dedicate?

A poet has said -

> **mera mujhame kucha nahi jo kucha hai so tor**
> **tera tujhako soupate kya lage hai mor**

All that I have belongs not to me but is Thine
What I dedicate to You has never been mine

King *Bali* asked God to claim the earth in three steps. God assumed a huge form and in just two giant steps covered the earth, the cosmos and heaven. He then asked King *Bali*, "Where should I put my third step?" *Bali* replied that till now, only the objects possessed by the owner had been offered, not the owner himself. He said, "Put your third step on my head because I am the owner of the earth and so I am greater than it". This was true, but *Bali* had coordinated his body, senses, breath, mind and intellect and had still retained his limited ego. He was therefore bound by *varuna pasa*.

Bali's wife *Vindhyavalī* prayed to God and implored, "Oh Lord! You have meted out the right punishment to my husband. The world is your playground. You have created it and it belongs to you. My husband was wrong in thinking that he owned what is rightfully yours". Hearing this, God set *Bali* free.

King Bali is the ordinary unawakened mortal and Vindhyavalī his wife is the saranagati. The saranagati releases the bound, unawakened mortal, King Bali symbolises a mortal and his wife Vindhyavalī symbolises one who goes into the shelter of the Lord. The one who goes into the shelter of the Lord gets liberated and he is free from bondage.

Chapter 2

THE NEED FOR REFINED INTERESTS

Seen from an ethical and spiritual viewpoint, society today is on the decline. We observe that neither the individual, the society, nor the country is satisfied with its current state. In fact, it doesn't even know what it really wants or where it is headed.

Ignorance of the true goal of life and delusions regarding the means to achieve it lead to confusion about one's direction in life.

Generally, after Man has had the experience of contentment achieved through different means, then the attainment of happiness becomes his greatest desire. This desire will not be satiated through small achievements. He wishes to permanently remove all obstacles in the way of attaining a permanent blissful state.

In reality, all living beings wish to be totally free from sorrow and attain eternal happiness. This being the greatest purpose of man, is the ultimate goal *purusartha* is the aim of the human life and it is divided in four parts which are *Kama*, *artha*, *dharma* and *moksa*.

With this purpose in mind, the wise men of the world perform various *karma*. However, it has been observed that this blissful state that Man strives for is always out of his reach and unwanted sorrows remain. For the attainment of any purpose, just determining the goal does not suffice. The means of achieving it should be appropriate. This is because the means is instrumental in attaining the righteous purpose, which is not possible by employing unrighteous means.

The wise men of our country, through experience and by following the *sastra* have ascertained that there is no greater happiness than that which lies in God.

Seeking happiness elsewhere is like running around in search for illusionary clean waters to quench your thirst, while all the time, the pure water lies hidden beneath the scum. God is happiness and lies deep within the heart of Man. Similarly, the true happiness that we seek, appears to be out of our reach because it is hidden deep inside our being.

Although this eternal happiness lies right within and is an integral part of the enlightened soul, the means and the different forms of its expression appear to make it distinctive. It is the means that make it appropriate or inappropriate.

The means of the expression of happiness is through a pure and calm soul. The reflection of the moon in the dirty waters of a lake will be unclear, but the same image will appear clearly in pure and still water. As the purity and stillness of the lake increases, the reflection will appear clearer and steadier. In the same way, the greater the purity and calmness of the soul, the clearer is the expression of happiness.

Depending upon the means of expression, happiness is differentiated into three types *visayananda*, *bhagavadananda* and *brahmananda*. It is a rule that the good and bad *karma* of Man will bear fruits which accordingly will be the cause of happiness or sorrow.

When a certain desire is aroused in the mind, it starts pricking him like a thorn and the person starts striving to attain the object of his desire. This desire gradually gains strength and gives rise to other desires. In such a state, when the desired object is attained (due to the involvement of the senses) there is a feeling of happiness and freedom from that particular desire.

This brings momentary purity and calmness in the soul. In such a state, the reflection of the eternal happiness is *visayananda*. However, due to the temporary nature of the *sattvika gunna* released from desire the dependency of the senses on the temporary euphoria experienced due to attainment of the desired object which makes this type of happiness transient, inappropriate and the cause of sorrow.

Lord *Krsna* says in the *Gita* that happiness borne of sensual or material pleasures is the cause of sorrow and asks the wise to renounce such pleasures. When Man strives for *bhagavadananda* and *brahmananda*, he will attain permanent happiness. *Vidurají* has suggested a wonderful means of attaining happiness:

ekaya dve viniicitya
trÍmscaturbhirvasÍ kuru
panca jitva viditva sat
sapta hitva sukhÍ bhava

"With a discerning and discriminating mind, decide what is eternal and what is temporary, then through *sama (self restraint)*, *dama* (restraint of the senses), *uparama* (focus) and *sraddha* (faith), bring *kama* (sexual desire), *krodha* (anger) and *lobha* (controlled greed). Keep the sense organs (ears, eyes, tongue, nose and the skin) under control. Understand hunger, thirst, sorrow, attachment, old age, death and free yourself from these. Uplift your soul above them through an understanding of the five sense organs, the mind and intellect. This freedom will give you happiness. The happiness attained through this means is not external. What is required is the elimination of that which obstructs it, from clear thoughts.

Bliss gained through detachment is greater than contentment through attachment. According to the *GÍta*, the devotee who renounces attachment for external objects experiences an extraordinary happiness within himself. He then, through *brahmasaksatkara* attains bliss permanently. The *Yoga texts* say:

"When pure thoughts pervade the soul through *samadhi*, the happiness that is attained cannot be expressed through words. It can only be experienced. In reality, as the mind of Man keeps getting purified, his interests too become refined. When the interests are refined, the beliefs regarding happiness change."

A village boy will think that jaggery is the sweetest thing he has ever tasted. But when he tastes sarkara, sÍta and kanda, he will no longer want to eat jaggery.

A person who once used to love folk songs, will no longer be enthralled by them when he becomes an expert of classical music. Poets and lovers of high literature have no fascination for simple folk songs. That is why, books on spirituality say that the happiness attained by the ascetic who has renounced the world and lives in seclusion, will never be experienced by emperors or even Lord *Indra*.

The *yogÍ* who has tasted the bliss of *brahmananda* will consider even Lord *Indra* to be a destitute.

Even Lord *Adi Sankaracarya* considers those who are free from passion and who delight in the utterances of the *Vedanta*, to be fortunate - *KaupÍnavantah khalu bhagyavantah* : "The happiness derived from sensual pleasures of this world and the greater happiness attained in the other world as a result of our good *karma*, even when combined together do not measure up to the bliss experienced through the destruction of desires."

The *bhutabhavana visvanatha sadasiva* Lord *Sankara* used to keep the company of ghosts and demons, wear a garland of skulls around his neck and smear his body with ash. All this shows that regardless of external circumstances as happiness lies within us, not outside. It lies in renunciation, not in procuring and seizing. *Maharsi Vasistha*, in the *Yoga-Vasistha*, tells us to make Lord *Rama* our ideal to attain happiness.

The *paramapada* that remains after warding off *asesa visesa* all the distinctions through *neti-neti* "Not this Not this", and which cannot be given any form, is you. Understand this and you shall be happy. The resolution and steadiness of the heart like a rock (but not lifeless) is *paramapada*.

Ardent devotees who have experienced happiness through devotion of *druta-citta* say "Oh Lord! The joy that one experiences when one hears the words spoken by Your devotees who praise Thy glory and benevolence, is greater than that of *brahma*. How can this happiness be attained by Gods who fall from a plane which has been broken open by the sword of time?"

After having met Lord *Rama*, King *Janaka* was so overcome by the love for *bhagavadananda*, that he willingly renounced *brahma sukha*. The other son of King *Dasaratha Bharata*, after completing *Prayaga*, the greatest of pilgrimages, renounced *artha*, *dharma*, *kama* and *moksa* and asked to be blessed with nothing except to serve Lord *Rama* and *Sita* in every birth.

In the *Ramacaritamanasa*, *Bhusundi*, (a devotee of Lord *Srirama* in the body of a crow) while speaking about the good fortune of the natives of *Avadhapuri* who used to continuously witness the *lila* of Lord *Rama*, says "the happiness for which Lord *Siva* used to put on a terrifying appearance, was experienced by natives of *Avadhapuri* at all times. Oh *Khagesa*! That happiness, if experienced just once by a person even in his sleep, was considered by him to be greater than *brahma-sukha*."

The essence of it is that *brahma-sukha* (an integral part of the soul) can be experienced only when the soul is made pure with a lot of effort through *samadhi*. However, when the soul is automatically permeated with the thoughts of happiness this is called *bhagavat-sukha*. This *bhagavat-sukha* is greater than *brahmasukha*.

This blissful state appeals to *BhusundÍ*, even if experienced through the body of a crow. Those whose sorrows have been destroyed by the reflection of the wonderful and ideal character of God, through whichever physical body that has been bestowed upon them, who delight in keeping the company of *satpurusa* or the virtuous men, find great happiness in *satsanga* and even renounce the desire for *moksa*. Those who are religious find immense joy in religious rituals and ascetics find the same in penance. Lord *Rama* considered fourteen years of *vanavasa* or banishment to the forest as per his parent's orders, to be more joyful than ruling over the empire of *Ayodhya*.

People, who are devoted to their country, find the happiness of serving their country and facing hardships for it, to be greater than domestic happiness. Some people happily lay down their lives and face the gallows for the sake of their country.

A married woman relinquishes her personal happiness and devotes herself to serving her husband. She finds extraordinary happiness in it. This, as per the *GÍta*, is *sattvika sukha* or *sattvika* happiness. This initially may feel as though one is drinking poison, however, it eventually bestows great bliss and the poison turns out to be nectar. This is possible only through purification of the soul.

The means of soul purification are *svadharmanusthana* (performing one's own duty imposed by the birth, the stage of life in society), *sadacara* (conduct of the virtuous people), *satsanga* (the company of the saints), *Acaryopasana* (it is the meditation and the method of realization given by the master), *sama* (control of the mind), *dama* (control of the external senses), *uparati* (absence of distraction from the goal), *sraddha* (is the faith in the words of the *Guru* and in the teachings of *Vedanta*), *viveka* (discriminating factor), *vicara* (is the continuous reflection of the eternal truth as exposed by the teacher and the *Vedanta*), *antarmukhata* (is the natural tendency of the virtuous).

Today man, has forgotten this path and is hopelessly wandering around.

To make an individual, society, the nation and the world happy, Man needs to change his beliefs regarding happiness. Not only should he respect and not disregard the traditional, cultural, religious, ethical and spiritual values of his homeland but they should also follow these in every aspect his life and bring about a radical change in their actions.

Accordingly, he should set up a daily regimen. *Samskara* lie inherent within Man.

What is required is the initiation of a large-scale movement to purify the thoughts for their awakening.

Chapter 3

MAKE DHARMA AND PARAMARTHA-CHINTANA YOUR RESOLVE

According to the *srímadbhagavadgíta*, nature and the soul are eternal. Since time immemorial, this soul has been trapped in the cycle of birth and death. In each birth illness, sorrow, old age and death are inevitable. Those who consider life to be the period between the birth of their present body and its death are absolutely unaware of the fearsome cycle of births. Only those who understand that their lives are nothing but the continuation of the eternal and endless soul, are aware of this and with this awareness, they can comprehend the endless cycle of birth, illness and death. They wonder as to why they did not try to attain *moksa* in spite of countless births. In reality, the attraction towards material attachments, worldly pleasures and desires, are obstacles to thought and devotion. It is due to these that Man turns away from *moksa* (emancipation) and instead desires sensual pleasures, wine and women.

Oblivious of its true self due to the confusing jugglery of nature, the soul cannot understand that which one perceives as happiness is actually a cause of sorrow. *Maharsi Patanjali* has said in the *Yogasutra* -

Parinama-tapa-samskara-duhkhairgunavrttirodhacca duhkhameva sarvam vivekinah

In other words, due to the conflict between the sorrows arising out of *tapa samskara* and the state of the *guna*, everything appears sorrowful to the discerning eye. The world is always changing. Except for the soul, all things tangible as well as intangible keep changing.

The process of change is very subtle and cannot be easily grasped. In the same way, due to our wide perspective, we are unaware of finer and subtle changes like the ripening of the fruit in the mango blossom, which, from the size of a mustard seed grows into a big juicy fruit. If seen from this perspective, our happiness is temporary due to the destructive results of sensual pleasures on our senses and our body which strenuously strives for it. Along with this, due to Man's absorption in divine, worldly and spiritual *tapa*, he always remains deprived of happiness in this world. Hardships caused due to *prarabdha karma* and adverse planetary effects, the conflict between people and unexpected accidents, suffering caused due to physical illnesses and mental distress are called *tritapa*. Even the most delicious food tastes insipid when one is suffering from fever. Similarly, all types of happiness become meaningless due to these three *tapa*. When Man experiences words, touch, appearance, taste and smell which delight his senses, the resultant happiness that it evokes is temporary and hence destroyed. However, the nature of desire remains and keeps causing anguish. Man, attracted by the beauty of a rose in a garden, plucks it, admires it, smells it, touches it and when it withers, crushes it and throws it away. Similarly, happiness is short-lived but the pain caused by thorns that pricked the fingers whilst plucking the rose, endures for quite some time. In this way, an inclination towards pleasure, change in desires, inability to fulfill them or after they are destroyed, cause great anguish and suffering. Due to the effect of the nature of the three *gunas - sattva*, *rajas* and *tamas*, the interests and desires of Man keep changing. When the desire for a certain object arouses, the feeling it evokes in the heart at that time does not remain the same when it is attained after striving long and hard for it. The eagerness towards it and the enjoyment for it does not remain. This too, as a result, causes anguish.

For this reason, the person who is judicious and discerning understands that worldly pleasures are nothing but the cause of unhappiness. His focus changes from the striving to attain such transient happiness to the search for true happiness.

Some modern day psychologists claim that trying to turn oneself towards asceticism represses the instinctive and natural desires of a person and due to the restrictions it imposes, results in the development of psychological disorders and complexes. However, this cannot be called a rational claim. This is because when one reflects upon and realizes the vileness of desires, one automatically becomes detached from them. There is no repression, just freedom from desires. Detachment does not mean disappointment; it means the turning of the mind away from worldly matters. It is said that sex is a natural and instinctive desire in all living beings. However, the fact that they also instinctively desire freedom, cannot be accepted because freedom cannot be attained if there is dependency on material and sensual pleasures for happiness. Desires make

Man its slave. The eternal soul has had the good fortune of being reborn as a human being for countless birth. However, in spite of being blessed with the human form, Man has not done what he should have done. The human body is capable of performing deeds that other forms of life are incapable of performing. According to our *Sastras*, of the eighty four lakh *yoni* or reincarnations, only the human reincarnation is *karmayoni*. The rest are all *bhogayoni* (desires). This is the reason why the human form is of greater importance than that of God. Humans are capable of attaining the four *purusartha* or goals-*artha*, *dharma*, *kama* and *moksa* and according to some, even the fifth goal of love (devotion). Except for *dharma*, all these goals are fruits. *Dharma* is devotion as well as fruit. *Dharmacarana* or religious observance differentiates the human body, senses and all the strivings of the mind into *dharma* and *adharma*. In other words, our diet, daily activities, what we speak, hear, see and think, all become *dharma* or *adharma*. Our strivings, if in accordance to the *sastras*, are *dharma* and if in conflict with them, are *adharma*. We can, if we so wish, easily turn them into *dharma*.

We have wasted countless births that we have been given by either dedicating ourselves to the fulfillment of our desires for our enjoyment or becoming the means of enjoyment for others.

We must resolve that in this birth, we will dedicate our life to *dharma* and *paramartha cintana*. We will give up bad company and do *satsanga*. We will, through reflection and meditative thinking, detach our mind from sensual pleasures and devote it to the gentle, pure, benevolent and easily attainable *caranakamala* or the Lotus feet of God. Having had the manifestation of *paramatattva* or the Supreme Truth, we will free ourselves of all worldly attachments. We will dedicate every moment of the rest of our life to the welfare of others.

Chapter 4

GOD FAVOURS DHARMA

According to our *sastras*, the human form, being capable of *dharmacarana, bhagavad - bhajana* and *brahma* is considered to be the superior most of the 84,00,000 species of beings. Similarly, of the four goals-*dharma*, *artha*, *kama* and *moksa*, *dharma* is considered to be the superior most.

This is because *dharma* is the cause of *artha, kama, dharma* for other worldly happiness and *moksa*.

The *sastras* have an ascertained principle that virtues and good deeds of the past life bestow *artha* in this life and the combining of the senses with the appropriate words-touch-appearance-taste-smell, bestow happiness. When the soul leaves the body, it does not take any kind of material possession with it. What goes with it is the *dharma* it has performed. It is in this way, by renouncing the desire for fruit and by *dharma* performed with a *bhagavatpada-pankaja-samarpana* mind, that *moksa* can be attained through *bhagavadbhakti* and *tattvajnana*.

God created this world and for its protection, created *Marĺci* and other kings and instructed all to perform *pravrttilaksana dharma* as per the *Vedas*. He also created *Sanaka, Sanandana, Sanatana* and *Sanatkumara* were the first four human beings created by Lord *Brahma*, who were supposed to start the entire creation of the race of humans but as they did not want to do it, they till today exist in their immortal life, which called for *nivrttidharma jnana* and asceticism. There are two types of *Vedic dharma – pravrttilaksana* and *nivrttilaksana*. (according to *pravrttilaksana* follow the *veda* and live your life as per *varnasrama* (*Brahmacarya, Grhastha, Vanaprastha* and *Samnyasa*). *Dharma* is to follow your life as per the four *asrama* and practice *yama* and *niyama*. *nivrttilaksana* (In this stage one has fulfilled all desires and the only desire left is the desire for liberation). Only those whose souls have been purified by performing *pravrttilaksana dharma* are deserving of *nivrttilaksana dharma jnana* and asceticism.

If Man thoroughly understands the nature of *dharma* through the *sastras* and by keeping the company of virtuous men, he can turn his body, senses and all the strivings of his mind into *dharma*. This is because when these strivings are in accordance to the *sastras*, they become *dharma* and when they go against the *sastras*, they become *adharma*.

If we so wish, we can turn all that we see, hear, speak, eat, drink and think into *dharma*. But this would require us to have full faith in the insightful Creator and the *Vedas* that He has prescribed. An intelligent person will easily understand that the omniscient Almighty God who has created the whole world, encourages *dharma* because following *dharma* is beneficial to the soul. Only by following *dharma* can the soul be awakened and attain *moksa*.

"*Yatodharmas tato jayah*" This principle indicates that God encourages *dharma*. The question now arises that why doesn't Man have faith in *dharma* and the *sastras*? The *Skandapurana* (There are eighteen *purana* and *Skandapurana* is one of them which describes the religious history of ancient history of India, which has no begining and was written by *Veda Vyasa*, who was the son of *Rsi Parasara* and *Satyavati*) attributes this to the presences of physical, verbal and mental vices-

> **Adattanamupadanam**
> **himsa caivavidhanatah**
> **paradaropasevaca**
> **sarÍram trividham smrtam**
> **parusyaanrtan caiva**
> **paisunyancapi sarvasah**
> **asambaddhapralapasca**
> **vanmayam syaccaturvidham**
> **paradravyesvabhidhyanam**
> **manasanista-cintanam**
> **vitathabhinivesasca**
> **manasam trividham smrtam**

"Forcibly seizing other's possessions, violence directed towards living creatures and keeping sexual relations with another's wife are the three physical vices. Speaking harsh words, lying, slandering others and idle chattering are the four verbal vices. Scheming to procure other's wealth, evil thoughts and stubbornness are the three mental vices. All these add up to ten vices. These ten vices are responsible for Man's disbelief and lack of faith in God."

The virtuous should renounce these vices. Today, the pride that people take in being an atheist and ridiculing religious belief is due to the presence of these vices.

Sanatana (eternal) *dharma* permits us to worship six forms of God. *Ndi Sankaracarya* is called *sanmatasthapanacarya*. The *nirguna nirakara* (the unqualified, formless Ultimate Being), the *saguna sakara (the qualified incarnate), both forms can be worshipped as God. There are five kinds of saguna sakara Siva, Sakti, Ganesa, Surya and Visnu. actually there is no difference between them. They are just different names of one God who assumes different roles like an actor for the deliverance of his devotees. Worshipping one is equivalent to worshipping all. When the nirguna nirakara is also worshipped along with these five, they add up to six.*

Though the *kartavya* (duties) *karma* (action) are differentiated into *varna, asrama, vaya* and *avastha*, their measure, purpose and basis are the same. Lord Krsna, in the sixtenth chapter of the *Srimadbhagavadgita*, has classified Man into two types: *daivi* (good virtues) *sampad* and *asuri* (opposite of good virtues) *sampad*. A revelation says -

"Dvaya ha prajapatyah devas casuras ca"

Daivi sampad is fearlessness, *sattvasamsuddhi* (soul purification), *paravancana* (listening to the discourses of the saints and the wise, avoiding maya and falsehood or, in other words, conduct with pure intentions), appropriate *jnanayoga* (understanding the true nature of the soul with the help of the *Sastra* and a guru or teacher and experiencing it with a focused mind and having full faith in it), *dana* (generously distributing food), *dama* (keeping the senses under control), *tapah* (penance), *ahimsa* (non-violence), *satya* (truth), *akrodha* (dissolution of anger), *tyaga* (renunciation), *santi* (peace), *apaisuna* (not slandering others), compassion for all living creatures, keeping the senses impassive in spite of the presence of pleasures, gentleness, shying from bad karma, steadfastness, determination, forgiveness, keeping the body and senses alert, purity, absence of ill-will and humility. *Asuri sampad* is deceit, arrogance, pride, anger, speaking harsh words and refusal to acknowledge one's *kartavya* (duty).

The strongest foundation for *dharma* is avoiding *asuri sampad* and making the *sadguna* of *daivi sampad* a part of our life. Without this, some *religious* activities end up being mere means of livelihood and sometimes, not even that.

The *srimadbhagavadgita*, in addition to *daivi sampad*, also speaks of calmness and the qualities of the *bhagavadbhakta* as well as the unqualified Supreme Being. Lord Rama (in the *Ramacaritamanasa*) speaks of the characteristics of ascetics. All these are ideals of virtuous and religious men.

The natural state of ascetics becomes a means for devotees. *Ndarsa* (ideals) are mirrors. Just as the extroverted Man looks at himself in a mirror to enhance his appearance, so does the devotee look at the pure devotion and behaviour of highly virtuous men and strives for spiritual growth.

The superiority and inferiority of any karma depends upon the mental state of the *karta* (doer). This makes it necessary for him to maintain a superior mental state. All types of karma and worship require the above mentioned *sadguna* to the same extent.

In the *Srimadbhagavadgita*, Krsna says "I always walk behind devotees who are impartial, calm, peace-loving, reflective and objective in thought. By doing this, the dust of his feet can fall on my head and I can become purified." This shows the extent to which God respects sadguna.

Evidence says that Lord Srí Krsna, though close to both the Kaurava and the Pandava, chose to be the charioteer of *Arjuna*.

There are only two options that are faced by the traveller on the path of devotion: an awakening or a downfall. There is no room here for stagnancy and complacency. As an individual, Man will always remain incomplete during his entire life and he should endlessly strive to make himself complete. In reality, taking pride in being complete and becoming complacent, indicates incompleteness.

The ten characteristics of dharma are *dhruti* (resolve), *ksama* (forgiveness), *dama* (repression), *asteya* (refraining from stealing), *sauca* (purity), *indriya-nigraha* (control over the senses), *jnana-vijnana* (thorough knowledge), *satya* (truth) and *akrodha* (dissolution of anger). By employing these, Man can become human in the true sense of the word. Dharma purifies the mind and adharma makes it unclean.

Purity and contentment of the mind are one and the same. Our happiness and sorrows are closely related to our mind. This is the reason why those with an impure mind are always distressed and restless. The willingness, with which Man amasses material possession for happiness, is also required for the purification of his mind. Without this, Man's progress will be incomplete and he will never become truly happy.

Following *dharma* may initially pose some difficulties. However, they are not really difficulties. Those who live near the bank of the river *Ganga* and take a bath in it just before sunrise, during the month of *Magha* (This month corresponds to the month of January which is peak winter), may at first experience some distress due to the chilled water but the happiness experienced after the bath, are beyond description.

Those who follow *adharma* will meet with a grievous end. Due to their mental state, they will neither be able to love anyone nor will they find satisfaction in any circumstances. We must keep in mind the fact the God favours truth, justice, virtuous, moral conduct and remain resolute on the path of dharma.

Chapter 5

SOLUTION OF THE MIND

SOLUTION OF THE MENTAL PROBLEMS?

There are just two things in the world: the mind and the thoughts. That which thinks and reflects is the mind and that which is reflected upon are the thoughts. The mind devoid of thoughts is the consciousness (enlightened soul). The mind is always thinking about something. The mind through which many disconnected thoughts are always running, is an unsteady and wavering. The mind which uninterruptedly reflects upon a single thought is a focused mind. On deep reflection, one realises that the impurity and purity of the mind depends upon the impurity and purity of the object of contemplation. With this objective, Lord *Krsna* speaks to his friend *Uddhava* -

'Gunadosadrstirdoso
gunastubhayavarjitah'

"The consideration of virtues and vices is a vice in itself and virtue is to be free of the thoughts of the two." In reality, nothing is created or destroyed in the soul. The soul is consistent and unchanging. Any kind of irregularity or goodness occurs only in the mind. Therefore, we must concentrate on the purification of the mind. The purpose of *karma*, *upasana* and *yoga* is the purification of this mind.

When man performs *karma* which are made impure with the desire for objects to gratify the senses, or even contemplates them, his mind gradually weakens. After sometime, he loses control over his emotions, thoughts and his actions. He is then enveloped by a *parampara* of misfortune.

It is for the prevention of this weakening of the mind that the *sastras* and highly virtuous men have advised to perform highest *karma* and to worship God. From a philosophical point of view, the soul is a part of God. But when it forgets its true nature, it loses its divine qualities and becomes weak.

By meditating upon God which is the essence of our soul, we can be free from these. There is a famous *sloka* in the spiritual books -

> *Pranayamairdehadosan*
> *dharanabhisca kilbisan*
> *pratyaharena samsargan*
> *dhyanenatmÍvaran gunan*

"Burn all the vices of the body and mind through Pranayama, sins through *dharana*, worldly attachments through *pratyahara* (withdrawal of the mind from desires) and ungodly *gunas* qualities through meditation." This *íloka* speaks about the importance of spiritual devotion.

If the devotee attains a state of calmness through *siddhasana*, *padmasana* or *sukhasana*, practices sitting in these *asanas* for a long time and instead of trying to consciously inhale and exhale, just focuses on his normal breathing, then, after some time, *pranayama* is automatically achieved. This helps to focus the mind and meditate.

A crying baby is pacified by rocking the cradle. Similarly, our mind too is like a baby, which can be calmed by inhaling and exhaling which are akin to the rocking movements of the cradle.

Turmoil increases the restlessness of the mind. In such a state, neither are we able to eat well nor are we relaxed enough to fall asleep. We cannot even sit peacefully for *bhajana*.

Controlling the state of the mind is called *samadhi*. Stupor, agitation, irritation and delight are all obstacles to the practice of *samadhi*. Languor is stupor, restlessness of the mind is agitation, the smallest of desires are irritants and the joy experienced when the mind is collected is delight.

Over-eating, lack of sleep and working too hard cause stupor. A balanced diet and regimen should be followed to eliminate this. When the mind is in an agitated state, it needs to be awakened.

Lord *Ndi Sankaracarya* has said "On a balance, weigh the restlessness of the mind against good sense. On one side, keep all your desires and on the other, keep the thoughts of God and then decide what is more beneficial and helps you to relax. Your rationality and experience should help you decide and once you have come to a decision, you should follow it".

Irritation of the mind can be removed by a detached observation of the vices such as desire, anger and passion which are present in the mind. The tendency to see delight can be removed through becoming detached. If the *upasana* is earnest, it will naturally include *navadhabhakti* (the nine kinds of devotion), but *japa* and *dhyana* are of prime importance.

God can be worshipped in two forms: the unqualified, formless Ultimate Being and the qualified incarnate. If someone wishes to fill a well with air, all he has to do is remove the mud and water from it. Air does not have to be brought in from outside. It has always been present there. In the same way, worshipping the unqualified, formless Ultimate Being require only the elimination of all desires from the thoughts. Worshipping the unqualified, formless Ultimate Being becomes easier when one focuses one's thoughts on the union of the consciousness-unconsciousness and the process of inhaling and exhaling.

In order to worship the qualified incarnate, make *Siva*, *Sakti*, *Visnu*, *Ganapati* and *Surya* or any of their forms of your favoured deity, visualize their image in your heart and keep repeating their name. It also helps to remember your *guru* before you start your meditation.

Do not worry if your mind cannot concentrate for long during meditation. If a horse bolts, you should not run after it. You should approach it slowly and patting him gently, rein him. Similarly, the mind too should be brought under control gradually. If one keeps remembering the name of a deity, it is but obvious that the deity (whose name is being remembered) will always be present in the person's heart.

Just as embankments have to be made from far, right from the source of a river in order to direct its course, so does the turning of the mind require efforts to be made from far. It requires following of an appropriate routine and *sadacara* (virtuous behavior).

It is necessary to avoid those deeds which turn the mind away from devotion. Deeds of a distressing nature render the doer incapable of meditation. Their meditation is like that of a snake which always has its hood raised in anger.

Bhajana and meditation are necessary for worldly success too. This is because the higher the deeds of Man, the greater is his success. High deeds come from having good intentions and only those who have a balanced mind can have righteous intentions to make rightful decisions.

The thoughts of a person, who worships God daily with a calm mind, becomes pure. This is because, at that time, his mind is free from distressing vices such as anger, passion and desire.

Therefore, every individual should devote a few moments of their precious time to *bhagavadbhajana* (worship of the Lord) and meditation.

Chapter 6

THOUGHTS AND ACTION

Those who are religious are convinced that *satkarma* (good deeds) bear *satphala* (good fruits) and that *asatkarma* (bad deeds) bear *asatphala* (bad fruits). *Karma* is never *nisphala* (fruitless) and inconsequential. Therefore it becomes the duty of every virtuous person to carry out *satkarma* for his bright future. Thoughts and *karma* are inseparable.

janati ichati atha karoti

"First comes the awareness of a certain thing, then comes the desire for it and eventually, Man performs deeds as per the desire. The three stages are knowledge without knowing the person has no desire and without desire there is no action."

This is a general rule. Thoughts form the basis of *jnana* and thoughts also bring resolve. In this way, thoughts and *karma* are inter-connected. Those *karmas* which we consider as natural and necessary, cannot be hastily resisted or opposed by the thoughts. We involuntarily blink our eyes, inhale and exhale countless times. However, when the thoughts become firm and stable, everything can be brought under control. Our buddhi (intelligence) governs our thoughts. According to the *Srimadbhagavadgita*, there are three types of *buddhi* - *sattvika* (pure), *rajasa* (action) and *tamasa* (lethargy). The *sattvika buddhi* is characterized by an awareness of pravrtti - *kartavya* - *akartavya* - *bhaya* - *abhaya* as well as *moksa* and *bandhana* or confinement. *Sattvika buddhi* is *sadbuddhi*. *Sadbuddhi* is the mother of *sadvicara* (good thoughts). If, on one side of a balance are kept all the riches of the world and *sadbuddhi* on the other, *sadbuddhi* will far outweigh the riches; the *Gayatri Mantra* is nothing but a prayer to grant us *sadbuddhi*. Wrong knowledge or wrongful thinking is the cause of most of the unhappiness in Man. Due to wrong knowledge, Man, in spite of attaining everything he wishes for, will remain unhappy. This is because bad thoughts shut the eyes of understanding and render Man incapable of choosing the right path. Thus, all his decisions become far removed from reality.

This is detrimental to both *paramartha* and conduct. That is why, Man should be ever aware and strive to attain and safeguard *sadbuddhi* and *sadvicara*. Although one may have to take some risks with one's conduct, if the *buddhi* is impure, thoughts and action also become impure. In the future, this gives rise to a *parampara* (Series) of misfortunate deeds. Only those who make it a routine to wake up early for *upasana* or devotion, can attain a pure *buddhi*. *Sadvicara* can arise only when the *buddhi* is not invaded by desirous, angry and passionate thoughts. The decisions that are made with a distressed *buddhi* should not be implemented. First of all, an attempt should be made to free the *buddhi* of distress. One should then wait patiently for the *buddhi* to be totally purified.

Do not worry if the purification of the *buddhi* takes time. Wherever paths open up, carefully deliberate over which path is appropriate for you. Walking on an impulsively chosen path may consume greater time and effort. You may, by luck, chance upon the right path, but this *pravrtti* towards impulsiveness will prove to be sorrowful in the future. This way of selecting the path can be applicable to every *pravrtti*. *Sattvikata* of the *buddhi* strengthens the thoughts. Strength and nobility of thoughts purify *karma*. It is a universally accepted rule that when there is a change in purpose, *karmaphala* changes too. There is a decree - "consider not the quality and quantity of *karma*; rather, consider the *buddhi* behind the *karma* and whether the *karta* (doer) is deserving of the *karma*." *Karma* performed with *sattvika buddhi* increase the strength of the mind of the doer. It liberates him from shame and remorse. Only by performing such *karma* can Man prosper; such *karma*, to which one does not get attached and if need be can be given up.

This rule is also applicable to the thoughts. If there is attachment to thoughts and if one cannot give them up to attain a state of freedom from all thoughts, such a soul can never become a truly virtuous devotee. Healthy is the soul which is capable of freeing itself from thoughts and definite intentions. This state of the soul is possible only with an increase in the *sattvaguna*. This increase is the basis of all accomplishments.

It should be noted that regardless of an abundance of purity and virtue in the *buddhi*, true *jnana* can be attained only with the help of *pramana*. The means of attaining true *jnana* is called *pramana*. *srotra* (the ears), *tvak* (the skin), *caksu* (the eyes), *rasana* (the tongue) and *ghrana* (the nose) are the *pramana* for the actual *jnana* of *sabda* (words), *sparsa* (touch), *rupa* (form), *rasa* (taste) and *gandha* (smell) respectively. Estimation is considered to be the *pramana* for *paroksajnana* (*indirect jnana*).

The *buddhi* should take the help of the prescribed *pramana* for the *jnana* of a particular subject. The *buddhi* that turns away from the right *pramana* causes aimless wandering. The *buddhi* that is shrewd, free from anger, passion, impartial, capable of deciding what is appropriate and inappropriate and which takes the help of *pramana*, should be considered as the means of knowledge of the virtuous path and one should strive to attain such a *buddhi*. Some people consider their inner motivation to be the urging of God. However, one should keep in mind that such inner motivations can be achieved only with the appropriate *buddhi*. A mind which is full of desires will consider its desires to be the urging of God. It has been observed that a lot of people claim to have received urging from God but a greater part of the urging are but a reflection of their own feelings and desires. The *yogi* whose soul has been purified by devotion acquires visionary powers by which he can look into and know the past, present and future. However this cannot be categorised as *pramana*. This type of *jnana* can be considered to be real only when it is attained through appropriate *pramana*.

This type of visionary *jnana* is difficult to attain and only the greatest of devotees can attain it. One should not be proud of it.

The essence of it is that there should be a control over our *karma* by our thoughts, over our thoughts by our *sattvika buddhi* and over our *sattvika buddhi* by the *sastra*. Only then can we reach our goal through uninterrupted and endless devotion.

Chapter 7

CHOOSE SREYA

Ours is an highly spiritual country. Our ancestors from the beginning have been investigating the *paramatattva* or the Supreme spirit that has created this world. That Supreme Spirit which is unfettered by the bonds of time, matter and space. It is omni-present, eternal and intangible. In spite of extreme weather conditions of cold and heat our ancestors, without turning away from the woes of life which require being resolved, protected themselves from hunger and thirst, and endlessly pursued the quest for the highest goal of life.

The individual and society which protects this vast country of ours from various obstacles, by which our *samskrti - sabhyata* and *dharma* can sustain our living existence, is more or less spiritually inclined.

(explain *samskrti* or culture, *sabhyata* or civilization, *dharma* or religion).

Today, the world is absorbed in researching, producing, amassing and distributing various implements and means of pleasure and luxuries through the science of physics. According to our *Samkhya* philosophy (one of the six systems of philosophy), the threefold nature itself is instrumental in attaining the true goal of life. Science has transgressed its limits and greatly increased greed and desire in Man by paving the way for the ruthless exploitation of natural resources. As a result, Man has forgotten his true goal. Science may have taught Man to use the body, senses, intelligence and nature to its full capacity but science cannot help in sustaining and collective damage done due to this excessive exploitation of nature.

For example, the weariness that results from lack of sleep cannot be removed by inducing sleep with sleeping pills. This weariness and fatigue can only be eliminated through natural sleep. Let alone liberating us from old age and death, this materialistic science does not even have a solution for removing the impediment of the body and senses caused due to indulgence in pleasures and restoring it to its original healthy state.

The material pleasures of the world are limited and so is the capacity to enjoy them. It is impossible to experience eternal and infinite happiness through these pleasures. Just as the thirst of an elephant, in the scorching summer heat, remains unquenched by the water of a small lake, so does the thirst for happiness remain unquenched by sensual plesasures.

There is a story on *Naciketa* in the *Kathopanisad* (this *Upanisad* is part of the ten major *Upanisads* on which *Ndi Sankaracarya* has given commentaries)

Naciketa's father performed a *yajna* (sacrifice) and offered old unhealthy cows as *daksina* (is the remuneration of the priests who have performed the rite) to the *rsi*. Seeing this, *Naciketa* thought that a father's love for his son prevented him from offering the best cows. His father wanted to save them for *Naciketa*. But for the *yajna* to be performed in all sincerity, only the best should be given as offerings. To remind his father of this, *Naciketa* asked him, "To whom shall you offer me to?" When being asked this question repeatedly, his infuriated father said, "I shall offer you to death". Seeing his father's anger, *Naciketa* wept silently. He started thinking to himself "I am either one of the best or an average pupil amongst my classmates. I am definitely not a lowerranking pupil. Then why is my father offering me to death?" Nevertheless, he went to *Yamaraja's* house. *Yamaraja* (the Lord of death) was not at home at that time. *Naciketa*, going hungry and thirsty for three nights, sat in wait at *Yamaraja's* doorstep. When *Yamaraja* finally arrived and found a starving guest at his home, he was greatly distressed. He told *Naciketa* that he would be granted three boons for staying hungry for three nights. *Naciketa* firstly asked for his father's happiness. His second wish was for agni*vidya* (knowledge of fire). His last wish was to know whether life ceased to exist after death.

But *Naciketa* was already experiencing life after death. What he actually wanted to know was the true meaning of the soul which was very distinct from the body, senses, mind and intellect. *Yamaraja* tried to tempt him to ask for "immortality of your sons and daughters, ask for your own immortality, but do not ask me about death. Take this chariot, these horses and these beautiful women." Take all the means of merriment, revel in singing and dancing. But *Naciketa* passed the test. He said "sensual pleasures weaken the strength of the senses and of what use is an immortal life in which there is no peace and happiness. You may keep all the chariots, horses, beautiful women, pleasures and merriments with you. All I want is to know the true meaning of the soul."

On hearing this, *Yamaraja* was very pleased. He considered *Naciketa* to be deserving of *tattvajnana* (is the knowledge of the eternal reality) and giving him an appraisal of *sreya* (is the highest goal, beyond which one desires nothing) and *preya* (is what the human beings choose because it gives them sense enjoyments) said "that which is experienced by the senses, which initially seems to be happiness but which eventually brings sorrow, is *preya* and the eternal peace and happiness attained through *Atmajnana*, is *sreya*. An unintelligent person will choose *preya* but an intelligent one will choose *sreya*." Lastly, *Naciketa* attained true contentment when *Yamaraja* imparted *brahmavidya* to him.

It is necessary to look at the existing circumstances from our Indian perspective and evaluating them, combine them with spirituality.

Material happiness is an illusion. By hankering after it, do not transgress the limits of nature. Live a coordinated life which elevates the nature above deeds, bring pleasure and which encourages the attainment of *moksa*.

Grhasthasrama (householder's lifestyle) is where this coordination is done. Nowadays, there are so-called spiritualists who wish to convince people that they can, through their miraculous powers, fulfill people's desires.

However, if these miracles increase desire in Man, they go against spirituality. According to our spiritual *sastras*, they are considered to be obstacles. Only by overcoming these obstacles can one reach the higher levels of spirituality.

Our philosophy is all-encompassing. It incorporates *karma*, *upasana* and *yoga* and *jnana*. We should, as per our interest and capacity, choose a path and at all times, try to progress towards *sreya*.

We should not disregard the science of physics. We should understand its limits and make the best use of it without expecting more than what we are capable of achieving. We should not get carried away by it. Under no circumstances should man lose his good judgment. Life is full of ups and downs and the ones hardest hit are those who are not wise.

Intelligence lies in being absolutely cautious. Through it, we can analyze and discriminate over what we see and free ourselves of all confusion.

Chapter 8

DHARMA: THE ONLY SOLUTION FOR PREVENTING DECLINE OF ETHICAL VALUES

Dharma visvasya jagatah pratistha According to these words, this world is founded on *dharma*. It is *dharana* that safeguards mankind and keeps it ideally controlled as well as organized. *Dharma* establishes proper coordination between the individual, society and is thereby instrumental in the welfare of both.

Our *sastra* have laid emphasis on certain observances which, when implemented by the whole of mankind, can bring about its welfare. According to *Manusmrti*, *dhrti*, *ksama*, *dama*, *asteya*, *sauca*, *indriyanigraha*, *jnana*, *vijnana*, *satya* and *akrodha* are the *dharma* of Man. The *Srimadbhagavadgita* prescribes the following thirty characteristics of *dharma* for all of mankind "*satya* (truth), *daya* (compassion), *tapasya* (penance), *sauca* (purity), *titiksa* (forbearance), discrimination between what is appropriate and inappropriate, control over the mind, *ahimsa* (non-violence), *brahmacarya* (asceticism), *tyaga* (sacrifice), *svadhyaya* (self-study), *saralata* (simplicity), *santosa* (contentment), *samadarsI* (objectivity), service towards the Mahatmas, gradual renunciation of the desire for worldly pleasures, realization that acts of vanity bear evil fruits, *mauna* (silence), *Atmacintana* (selfanalysis), providing adequate food to all living beings, an unswerving belief in the existence of the soul and in God, *sravana* of God's endless benevolence and His *lIla* (His acts), *kIrtana* and *smarana* of His name, service towards Him, His *puja* (worship), *namaskara* (obeisance), *dasya* (devotion to Him), *sakhya* (considering oneself to be God's companion) and *Atmasamarpana* (total surrender to God). *Navadha bhakti* is also included in the above. Lord *Rama* (in the *Ramayana*) has imparted preachings of the *navadha bhakti* to *Sabari*: First is *satsanga*. Second is *kirtana* on stories of God's birth and deeds. Third is discussing the virtues of God. Fourth is expounding the preachings of God. Fifth is sincere service and devotion as per the counsel of our *Gurudeva*. Sixth is maintaining the purity of one's nature, exercising self-restraint and dedicatedly worshiping God. Seventh is *mantrajapa* (recitation of the *mantra*). Eighth is holding the devotees of God in the highest of regards and considering all living beings to be a form of God. Freedom from worldly desires and attachments, abundance of restraint and self-control. Ninth is contemplation of the true nature of the soul. *Navadha bhakti* (nine forms of devotion *smaranam*, *kirtanam*, *visnoh*, *Atmanivedanam*, *padasevanam*, *arcanam*, *vandanam*, *dasyam*, *sakhyam*) is also the means of *premalaksana bhakti* (a devotion of love).

All humans have an equal right to follow the above *dharmas*. They are free from any kind of discrimination. Today, due to his greed for material pleasures and wealth, Man has turned away from *dharma*. This has resulted in him being perpetually discontented and unfocused. And when disillusionment with the world sets in, Man tries to seek solace in *dharma* or pious *Mahatmas*, but his greed remains. *Dharma*, undoubtedly, is like the *kalpavrksa*. That which is wished for, is always fulfilled under the *kalpavrksa* (the tree in heaven that fulfills all our desires). The *tyaga* and *tapah* of true and pious *Mahamas* can also help in mitigating the miseries of mankind. But who can change a miserable world that recognizes no God? In reality, only a soul that has been made pure by carrying out detached *karma* can be truly happy and find peace.

Regardless of the prosperity Man attains or the wealth he accumulates, he will never experience true peace if his mind is lacking in purity. The spiritual *sastras* say -

> ***Yacca kamasukham loke***
> ***yaccadivyam mahat sukham***
> ***trsnaksayasukhasyaite***
> ***kalam narhanti sodasIm***

"The sensual pleasures of this world and the divine happiness of the other world, when added together, do not measure up to even one sixteenth of the happiness attained through the elimination of desires."

Lord *Sankaracarya*, in a questionnaire, has said -

> ***Trsnaksayah svargapadam kimasti?***

"What is *svargapada?*" The answer is: elimination of desires.

Modern-day critics have stated that are our Indian *sastras* and the thoughts of virtuous people are inconsequential and thereby, are the cause of the material downfall of our country. According to them, an increase in desire are essential for the attainment of any goal. However, upon reflection, one realizes that more than philosophical thoughts, it is the excessive desire and greed of the ordinary man that makes him idle and worthless. And it has been specified by those who have written the *Gíta* that idleness cannot be the means of purification of the soul.

Lord *Srí Krsna* states in the *Gíta* "you are entitled to *karma*, but not to the fruit. Do not let *karma* borne of the desire for fruit be the cause of your bondage and do not let idleness set in, for idleness is the cause of evil."

On the other hand, when Man's desire increases excessively and his faith in God and *dharma* weakens, he starts performing misdeeds. Once envy and hatred overpower him, he forsakes justice, righteousness, hard work, the true goal of life and starts chasing this illusionary happiness. As a result, the society as well as the individual undergoes a moral decline. This increases dishonesty and wickedness. Then Man stops at nothing to fulfill his despicable self-interest.

Today, we are an independent nation. We are free to develop it as per our wishes, yet, the decline in moral and ethical values in the country is intensifying. The hostile elements in the country and society are increasing. This is the reason why we are plagued by innumerable problems to which we are unable to find solutions.

The fact is that unless the individual desire for worldly pleasures is not brought under control, the society will not be free of violence, hatred, anger and envy. This task cannot be made possible without spirituality and *dharma*.

It is strange that today, the individual or the society wants to use religious sentiments as a means to further personal or political interests but does not want to implement or follow the same. Unless we make *dharma* an integral part of our lives, it cannot benefit us in any way. Our country needs people who are willing to sacrifice their all for the country. But can we expect this of people who do not follow the right *dharma* in life?

Spirituality is not against material prosperity or ambition for the same. But it does ask of us to take the path of *dharma* in attaining prosperity. Man should not allow prosperity to make him vain. He should, as per *dharma*, be generous in sharing the benefits of prosperity with others.

Man today, needs to change the definition of happiness. He should realize that greater than the happiness obtained by satiating his own appetite with delicious food, is the happiness attained by feeding a starving person, for God lies in the fire that burns in the stomach of that starving person. The one who has a pure soul is not dependent on external conditions for happiness. Happiness for him does not lie in procuring or seizing things but in *tyaga* or sacrifice. On the other hand, a person with an impure heart forever seeks luxuries and pleasures. But one does not always get what one wishes for and therefore such a person always remains discontented and unhappy. Mankind, which has been led astray in the tumult of present-day circumstances, should reevaluate its spirituality, *samskrti* and *dharma* and let them guide it through life.

Chapter 9

THE WELFARE OF ALL LIES IN GIVING UP BUDDHIVAD AND BECOMING BUDDHIYOGI

The spiritual books say -

avicarakrto bandhah

vicarena nivartayet

In other words, bondage lies in lack of thought and the way to liberation is through thought. The solution to all problems can be obtained through profound thinking.

Today, there is no dearth of thoughts. However, many problems still persist. This is due to the fact that rather than thinking for themselves, people mostly think for others. The fact is that each person should think for himself.

Observing silence is of great importance in spiritual devotion because when the occasion arises, we can reflect upon the extent to which we are able to implement all that we have thought of.

Glib academicians can (through skilled reasoning and logic) prove the world to be deceptive and also provide clarifications to any doubts that are raised against it. What remains to be seen is that for how long they can keep up this deception.

Various thoughts run through the mind of Man. However, only the thoughts which strengthen Man's resolve and which are put into action have the power to influence his life. This is because spiritual growth cannot come from a few random moments of discussion but requires a lifelong dedication towards it.

Most people are of the view that by carrying out *dharma* in this life through *sadhana* and *satsanga* is the means of attaining joy, peace and happiness. This attainment is possible only in the next birth. However, this is a biased view.

If we wish, we can, through these spiritual means, enrich our present lives too and bring happiness to it.

We ourselves are responsible for most of the complicated problems that arise in our lives. It is the absence of thought that gives rise to them. If Man clearly defines his purpose in life and the means to achieve it, if he curbs his impulsiveness and follows the right means to achieve his purpose then it would be easy to find solutions to most of the problems. This is possible only if the mind is made free of lust, anger, greed, inebriation, attachment, envy, hypocrisy and hatred.

The mistake lies in the fact that we are firstly unable to decide upon our purpose in life and then, even if we are well aware of our purpose, we forsake the means and end up causing self-destruction. For example:

A lot of people wish to bring peace to their domestic lives and also to be in the good books of friends and relatives. However, their actions are such that they end up destroying everything. When faced with the reaction of others, we sometimes acknowledge our mistakes and try to correct them or, at times, we are unable to even identify our mistake, let alone correcting it. This causes a lot of upheavals in the marital, social and political life. All people carry out *karma*. When asked why they work, they reply "if we do not work, what will we eat?" Then, if asked why they eat, they reply "to live." And when asked why they live, they reply "we live so that we can work and eat." But this is the wrong answer. The purpose of life is something altogether different from this. These questions and answers also reveal how many people eat to live and how many of them carry out *karma* to live.

Many people are out to amass wealth to make their lives happy but their greed increases to such an extent that they end up destroying their health and peace of mind. They forget that wealth is for the body and not the other way round. The means can never be the end or the goal. It is wise to give it lesser importance than the goal. If we are able to think in such a manner, we can find the solution to the main problem in our lives.

The visionary sages in the *Upanisads* have said -

na vittena tarpanĺyo manusyah

"Wealth cannot bring contentment to Man."

Worldly pleasures are transitory. They wear out the senses. However long life may be, it is still too short.

When *Yamaraja* tried to tempt *Naciketa*, the latter said-

"svobhava martyasya yadantakaitat
sarvendriyanam jarayanti tejah
api sarvam jĺvitam alpameva
tavaiva bahyastava nrtyagĺte"

The children and grandchildren, merriment, wealth and long life that you wish to bestow me with are all transitory and consequently, will only bring sorrow. A long life too cannot bring happiness. Therefore, I do not wish for all this. You can keep them with you."

Unless Man, who has been blinded by the dazzling brilliance of science and modernism, does not embrace the sages' perspective of life, his wandering will never end. It is only by abandoning the materialistic perspective that we can purify our personal, social and political lives.

The thirst for pleasures has greatly influenced the youth of today. Many so-called thinkers, by trying to establish the appropriateness of material desires, are adding fuel to the fire.

In reality, the natural tendency of all creatures, borne of desire, does not require preaching.

Preaching is required by those who do not have this natural tendency.

Who has taught the birds and animals about sensual pleasures? What is required is to correctly channelise and control these tendencies. This is exactly what dharma does. Lord *Srī Krsna* tells *Bharata* in the *Gīta* -

Dharmaviruddho bhutesu
kamo'smi bharatarsabha.

"Sexual desire, to the extent permitted by *dharma*, is a form of me. Wealth too, is not vile. However, it should be amassed as per *dharma* and for the purpose of *dharma*. *Dharma* teaches us to pursue material and sexual pleasures in limited measure."

The control of the mind and senses are also essential for the enjoyment of pleasures. It is necessary to always follow the rules. Feelings of hostility, envy, hatred and violence increase as the thirst for material and sensual pleasures increases. This will also have a detrimental effect on the love we feel for each other. If we disregard our Indian philosophy of life and let the greed for individual and social prosperity get the better of us, we will go astray. This is exactly what is happening today. The *buddhivadis* (those who rationalize) are many, but *buddhiyogīs* are few. Lord *Krsna*, by imparting the preaching of *buddhiyoga*, empowered *Arjuna* who was a *buddhivadī*.

If we wish to bring about purification in our conduct, we must keep in mind, the highest goal of our life: the realization of God. We must establish this goal in all areas of our lives and constantly maintain the coordination between the means and the goal. We must closely monitor our actions and feelings to make sure that they do not take us onto the wrong path.

We must, relinquishing all temptations and distractions, carry out the means to attaining our goal in life with full earnestness.

Chapter 10

HE WHO INTROSPECTIVES
IS A TRUE HUMAN BEING

Of the eight hundred thousand incarnations, it is the human incarnation that is the most superior. This is because other forms of life are totally dependent on nature. The human brain is highly developed due to which it can discriminate between what is appropriate and inappropriate, right and wrong and can hence carry out every action after deliberation. This is the reason why the rules-prohibitions of the *sastras* are applicable to humans. These rules prohibitions are not meant to take away Man's freedom but to set him free in the true sense of the word. If Man is unaware of the true meaning of *dharma-adharma*, happiness and sorrow, the darkness of his ignorance will give rise to difficulties. Therefore, in order to attain one's true goal, a thoughtful person should follow the wise counsel of elders and instructions given in the *sastra*.

The most important objective of every living being is to bring an end to all sorrows and to attain eternal happiness. To achieve this purpose, people keep making efforts but the results have always been found to be contrary. This is because the correct goal cannot be achieved by incorrect means.

Generally, all living beings desperately seek worldly pleasures for happiness and consider the attainment of these pleasures to be true happiness. However, this notion is a delusion. The judicious person is above all this. He observes that, that which is the object of desire, brings happiness when attained.

At first, desires are aroused and when sensual pleasures are indulged in, they become a source of happiness. Desire increases rapidly and till the time the object of desire is not attained, it remains the cause of unhappiness. When there is indulgence in pleasures, gratification is achieved and there is a momentary sense of satisfaction. But after this transient experience is over, desire increases and once again becomes the cause of dissatisfaction and unhappiness. Habitual indulgence in pleasures cannot free the senses of desire because indulging in them arouses the senses further. In addition, when happiness is experienced, one automatically starts hating that which brings unhappiness. Hatred causes suffering. The reason for the hatred is the fear of unhappiness. But it is impossible to permanently elude that which may take away our happiness. In such a state, unhappiness is inevitable. In addition, due to our bitterness, unless we hurt others with our thoughts, speech and actions, we will not be able to experience any pleasure. This, then, becomes *adharma* and in the course of time, becomes the cause of unhappiness.

The mind of Man lacks consistency. The three *guna* of the mind - *sattva*, *rajas* and *tamas*, which give rise to happiness, sorrow and desire, are, at times, aroused and at times, in a subdued state. Due to this, a thing that once was the cause of happiness becomes the cause of unhappiness. As a result, in spite of attaining that which is desired for, after striving hard for it, Man is never able to experience happiness.

But not everyone can understand this. Only the one who has a pure soul can understand the unhappiness that pleasures eventually bring. It has been said in the *yogadarsana* that the soul of a *yogī* is like the eyeball. Just as a spider's web is enough to irritate his eye, so does the pure heart of a wise man, perceive worldly pleasures as the cause of unhappiness.

The quest of a wise person makes him transcend pleasures. In his search for true happiness, he seeks guidance from spiritual *sastras* and the teachings of great philosophers. The spiritual *sastras* say that happiness attained by the elimination of all desires cannot be equaled by that attained through worldly pleasures, leave alone divine pleasures.

It has been said -

> *yacca kamasukham loke*
> *yacca divyam mahat sukham*
> *trsnaksayasukhasyaite*
> *kalam narhanti sodasīm*

In other words, the sensual pleasures of this world and the divine happiness of the other world, when added together, do not measure up to even one sixteenth of the happiness attained through the elimination of desires. Lord *Sankaracarya*, in a questionnaire, has said-

Trsnaksayayah svargapadam kim asti?

In other words, what is *svargapada*? The answer is elimination of desires.

The truth is that we embody happiness. The happiness experienced when one is in a state of unconsciousness during deep sleep is definitely not desirable. This is because at that time, the body, senses and the mind are all inactive. And when these are inactive, pleasure cannot be experienced. Yet, there is a feeling of happiness, and it is so extraordinary, that without it, Man would go insane. An insane person cannot sleep.

Happiness experienced during a state of unconsciousness is accompanied by ignorance. Therefore, in order to experience this happiness, a spiritual devotee renounces sleep and tries to attain it through *dhyana*, *samadhi* and *Bhagavadbhajana (worship of the Lord)*. Lord *Srí Krsna* says in the *Srímadbhagavadgíta* - the happiness of the soul, experienced by the devotee who is detached from worldly pleasures is eternal for the *brahmanistha Mahatma*. Learned scholars have said that the *samadhinistha* have the joy of experiencing *pratyagatma (the soul that lives in each and every person)*, whereas the great philosophers are able to experience the eternal happiness of *pratyakcaitanya (paramatma*, the supreme being) which is but a part of the indestructible, eternal, formless *Brahma*.

Once this happiness is attained, it encompasses all the worldly pleasures that one desires for. Just as the water in a well, pond or a lake is insignificant compared to the vast oceans into which water flows in from all directions, so do worldly pleasures become insignificant when one has attained spiritual happiness. Once it is attained, there is nothing left to be desired. Such a devotee has attained true contentment.

Wisdom lies in renouncing those *karma* which, according to the *sastra*, are deemed inappropriate and carrying out the prescribed *karma* without the desire for fruit, reflecting upon the true nature of worldly pleasures, *satsanga* of the virtuous and holy men, practicing *sadhana* as per the instructions of the *brahmanistha sadguru* (one who is a realised person), striving to free oneself of desire, anger and passion, understanding the worthlessness of materialism which eventually brings unhappiness, devotion to God and attaining enlightenment.

Man can make full use of his capabilities only when he stops following others blindly and becomes introspective. It is our good fortune to have been born as humans and we should therefore utilize our human body for purposes that cannot be achieved by other forms of life.

The human body is God's best creation. He has blessed us with it and we must always keep in mind that human life is like a quivering droplet of water on a lotus leaf, which can slide off the leaf at any time.

Chapter 11

THE SUCCESS OF SPIRITUAL DEVOTION LIES IN BELIEF

Unique from the body, life, mind and intellect, is the existence of the soul. Rebirth does take place. Heaven, *dharma-adharma*, are all true. God - the Lord of the world, *sarvakarana* (*one who is the cause for all that exists in the universe*), *sarvavyapI* (*one who pervades all*), *sarvabhutantaratma* (*one who is the inner self of all beings*), *sarvajna* (*one who knows all that exists*), *sarvasaktimana* (*one who is possessed all powers*), *karmaphalapradata* (*one who gives us the rewards of our actions, merits and demerits*), *akaranakaruna karunavarunalaya*, (one who is the ocean of compassion unconditionally compassionale) *nikhilaheyapratyanika* (negligent to all the avoidables), *acintyanantakalyana gunaganaikanilaya* (the only abode of the unconceivable, *endless host of meritorious virtues*), *sarvakarta* (*cretor of all*), *sarvabharta* (*protector of all*), *sarvaharta* (*destroyer of all*), friend of the poor, protector of the virtuous, punisher of the wicked, is also changeless, immortal, eternal, indestructible, *asabda* or having no sound, *asvarupa* or formless, *arasa* or having no taste, *arupa* or having no appearance, *agandha* or without any smell, *nirguna* or unqualified, *nirakara* or formless, *nirvikara* or changeless and *ekatmapratyayasara*. It was due to His urging that the *Vedamantra* manifested in the heart of *rsi-munis*. These collections of *mantras* are called eternal *apauruseya Veda*. The *rsis* did not create these *mantras*, rather, they had a manifestation of them. *Maharsi Krsnadvaipayana Vyasa* compiled these *mantra* and classified them into the *ägveda*, *Yajurveda*, *Samaveda* and *Atharvaveda*.

Sisyate hitam upadisyate anena iti sastram

45

According to this, the *Vedas* are the *sastras*. This is because they provide knowledge for the welfare of all living beings. The *Ramayana* and the *Mahabharata* are our history and an exposition of the *Purana Vedas*. In these, the principles of the *Veda* are explained through various stories.

Just as the ears are a standard for words, skin for touch, eyes for form, tongue for taste and nose for smell, so are the *sastras* considered to be a standard for *dharma* and the knowledge of *brahma*.

The *smrtis* (*dharmasastra*) formed by various *rsis* as well as the *puranas* (ancient history created by *Vyasa* and the *samhita* are part of the *veda* formulated by the *rsi*, all being in accordance with the *Veda*, are considered to be standards. Similarly, our *tantragranthas*, called *agama*, are also standards. The *granthas* created by God are called *agama*. These *agamas* give a detailed account of the various *mantras*, their *rsis*, *chanda*, the Gods and their *nyasa*, *dhyana*, methods of worship, *kavaca*, heart, *sahastranama* etc. These provide *artha* or wealth, *dharma*, *kama* or sexual desire and *moksa* as fruits. The *Veda* are divided into two parts - the *mantras* and *brahmanas*. They give an exposition of *karma*, *upasana* and *jnana*. They also reveal the secret behind various creations which has astonished even scientific thinkers in this age of physics. *Nyaya*, *vaisesika*, *samkhya*, *yoga*, *purvamImamsa* and *uttaramImamsa* are our six philosophies. Of these, *yogasastra* shows us the way to improve our physical and mental health.

The *upasana* section of the *Veda* is called *bhakti*. The word *bhakti* finds mention in the *svetasvatara Upanisad*. Since this is an *Upanisad* of the *mantra* section of the *Vedas*, it is called mantropanishad. There is a *mantra* -

> **yasya deve parabhaktir**
> **yatha deve tatha gurau**
> **tasyaite kathita hyarthah**
> **prakasante mahatmanah**

In other words, the Mahatma who worships his deity and likewise worships his guru, is the one in whose heart the meaning of the *Upanisads* is revealed.

All living beings desire happiness. Although happiness does not have any material form, the world inflicts unhappiness upon itself due to the desire for this material happiness. It prefers death over a life without happiness. According to the principles of the *Vedas*, happiness which has no specific attributes, is actually the inner soul. The soul is held dear by all. And that which is held dear, brings happiness. Therefore, happiness and the soul are one.

Happiness, which is the essence of the soul, is not material but lies in the consciousness. Ignorant are those who seek happiness in material pleasures. When the senses come in contact with the object of desire, the soul is contented and focused due to which there is a momentary expression of the soul. This is *visayananda* (happiness that comes from materials). The contentment of the soul attained through external means cannot endure. Therefore, attempts are made to bring the senses and the mind under control through *dharmacarana* and to bring about introspection. By doing so, the detached soul, indifferent to external pleasures, can experience its inherent happiness. It has been mentioned in the *Upanisads* -

> ### *yada pancavatisthante*
> ### *jnanani manasa saha*
> ### *vrddiica na vicesteta*
> ### *tamahuh paramam gatim*

In other words, when the mind, along with the five senses, is calm, the intellect too relinquishes thoughts of desire. This is called merging of the soul with the Ultimate Being.

This state is also called *nirvikalpa* or changeless *samadhi*. There is a continuous flow of this changelessness formed by the union of two instincts. Instincts are called *vikalpa*. Till the time the second *vikalpa* arises after the destruction of the first, there is a distinct awareness of the *nirviklapa* consciousness. This can be experienced by focusing the mind in the middle of *prana* and *apana* and in the middle of the state of complete unconsciousness and wakefulness. In the *yogavasistha*, when *Kagabhusundi* was asked - 'which God do you worship?', he replied -

> ### *pranapanayormadhye*
> ### *cidatmanam upasmahe*

In other words, it is the self-awareness lying between *prana* and *apana* (are the steps in *pranayama* which is the means to control your breath) that I worship. This is also called natural *samadhi*.

However, this kind of devotion requires *vairagya* or asceticism and subtlety of thought. this is not easy for the ordinary Man. *Raso vai sah* as per this revelation, happiness can also be called *rasa*.

According to the explanation given by historians, it is the consciousness that is *rasa-sabda-vacyah*. According to *Madhusudana Sarasvatī*, who was a *vedantic* if the permanent instinct be *SrĪkrsna*, it becomes *bhaktirasa* (if your keep repeating the thoughts will merge with him and you will have no other thoughts). It is evident that every human being longs for someone who he can love and who will reciprocate his feelings. Every individual definitely has some such person in their life. Yet, he remains disappointed because he always finds some kind of selfishness in others. The love that he feels towards others too is not unconditional or free from selfishness. Life without true love is insipid and meaningless. Death of loved ones, betrayal and physical incapability add to its meaninglsesness and hence one loses all zest for life. the only way to bring back this zest is by *bhagavadbhakti*. Where there is a feeling of *apantva*, i.e ownness there is love. The heart is filled with joy when it wells up with *bhaktirasa* due to the realization of the blessing that have been showered upon us when we invite God into our lives. *Navdhabhakti* is the basic means of *bhagavatprema* or love for God. By following this path, a number of householders as well as single men and women have been blessed with good fortune.

The *brahmakarata* (conversion in the form of Brahma) of the detached soul is called *jnana* and the *bhagavadakarata* (conversion in the form of the Lord) of the enlightened soul is called *bhakti*. The *rasa* in both cases is the same-*nirupadhika* is one and *sopadhika* in the other, both of which are *paramananda svarupa Atma* or the eternal happiness which is the essence of the soul. However, unless there is purification in the *karma ksetra*, the soul will not be conducive to the budding, growth, development and success of any kind of devotion.

For spiritual growth to take place, it is necessary for us to conform the desires of our body, senses, mind and intellect to the *sastras*. Actions refined through religious *samskaras* are called *samskrti*. Ideal conduct is called *samskrti*. The dharmic qualities of our actions are its adornments. The human reincarnation of *karmayoni* and all its desire becomes *dharma* and *adharma*. To lead a *dharmic* life, we must have belief. Belief is defined as *Vedokta dharmadharmesu visvasah astikyam*. In other words, that which the Vedas call *kartavya* is *dharma* and that which the Vedas call *akartavya* is *adharma*.

The soul of the person who has sinned physically, verbally or in thought, loses faith and belief. Therefore, it becomes extremely important for us to observe good conduct, avoid bad company, keep the company of virutous men and resolutely follow the path shown by them, which conform to the *iastras* and by means of *yoga*, *bhakti* and *jnana*, enlighten ourselves with the higher, higher and highest light of realization.

According to the immemorial Vedic *dharma*, of the unqualified and formless *Brahma*, *Siva-Sakti-Visnu-Ganapati* and *Surya*, anyone can be worshipped as a deity. The worship of God in any one of these six forms if called *sanmata*. Lord *Ndi Sankaracarya* has propagated the worship of these six forms of God. That is why he is called *sanmatasthapanacarya*.

Man, through his various desires, wishes to free himself from all sorrows and attain happiness. It is but natural that Man should wish for happiness. However, Man's desire for means of happiness is changeable and disorganized. Any worldly attachment to people and objects, which is a means to attaining happiness today, can become a hindrance in the way of attaining happiness tomorrow. Due to this, the fondness towards it starts changing. Many times in life, it happens that a person dislikes someone who was once very dear to him and starts liking someone who he once disliked. A friend turns into a foe and a foe turns into a friend. However, this state is that of the means of happiness, not happiness itself. Happiness can never be disliked. It is only due to the incorrect notion one has regarding the means of happiness that one feels desire for certain people and objects and hatred for certain others. According to the spiritual *sastras*, *prajnaparadha* (crime done knowingly) is the cause of all sorrows. *Prajnaparadha* is nothing but an inability to keep our mind pure and balanced. It is due to *prajnaparadha* or a lack of awareness of what is appropriate and inappropriaet that brings *adharma buddhi* to *dharma* and *dharma buddhi* to *adharma*. As a result, *pravrtti* where required, is absent, as is *nivrtti* from where it is required, absent. This is the reason why in spite of wanting happiness, sorrow is what Man finds. Therefore, it becomes necessary to eliminate *prajnaparadha*. It is *prajnaparadha* that makes us form attachments with others as well as break them. This is what has been happening since infinite births.

In reality, joy and sorrow are associated more with the mind than external means. External means can be a source of happiness as long as the mind is contented.

If the mind is discontented, no amount of appropriate words, touch, form, taste and smell can bring joy to it. Means of unhappiness to affect the mind greatly. Disease, unfortunate incidents, toil and separation from something which is dear are the four factors which cause physical suffering. Warding them off on time and not dwelling on them are ways of preventing sorrow. Therefore an intelligent Vaidya (physician) will first cure Man's mental unhappiness through soothing word and by providing appropriate remedies. Just like the cool water in an earthen pot will be heated by a piece of hot iron put into the water, so will the body suffer if the mind is full of sorrow. For this reason, just as a flame is put out by pouring water over it, so should one pacify the mind troubled with sorrows, with *jnana*. When the mind is free of sorrow, the body too will be free of suffering. The main cause of mental unhappiness is worldly attachments. Attachment causes fear and insecurity. The cause of sorrow, joy and suffering is also attachment. It is attachment that causes an inclination towards and love for pleasures. An inclination toward pleasures is considered to be the greatest cause of harm. Attachment destroys both *dharma* and *artha*. Desire is another word for attachment. It is responsible for arousing sexual desire and greed in Man. Man may wear out but his desires will not. None will be able to attain happiness unless desire is relinquished. Also, the mind cannot be made pure unless one renounces bad company. Man may escape unhurt by touching a flame but he will definitely get burnt if he touches red hot iron. The company one keeps evokes virtues and vices in Man. A number of *samskaras* lie inherent in the mind but conduct in accordance to them is possible only when they are aroused. The company one keep arouses these *samskaras*. It is a fact that the mind becomes depraved in the company of the depraved, mediocre in the company of the mediocre and greatly refined in the company of the highly virtuous.

The *jnana* of virtues and vices require purification of the mind. The one who has an impure mind will always tend toward impure things. However, highly virtuous men have a pure mind, keen discerning powers and their teachings are meritorious and their nature is to be emulated. When the vices of teh mind are elevated by renouncing bad company and keeping good company, one realises the meaning of true happiness and also the ways by which one can attain it. In reality, true happiness is form of God and the means of attaining it is by purification of the mind. The mind is essentially pure. Desire, hatred, sorrow, attachment and sexual desire make it impure. The impurity of the mind lies in its extroversion. Extroversion of the mind can be removed by *Bhagavatkathasravana*, *Bhagavadbhakti*, *samadamadi* and spiritual means. When the mind becomes introspective, it finds a wealth of happiness within itself. It then becomes contented and relinquishes all desires. This is called *mukti* (deliverance).

> **Mana eva manusyanam**
> **karanam bandha-moksayoh**
> **bandhaya visayasaktam**
> **muktyai nirvisayam manah**

In other words, the mind itself is the cause of bondage and deliverance. A pleasure seeking mind is the cause of bondage and a detached mind is the cause of deliverance. This is *paramartha* path and without understanding it Man will never be able to attain the true goal in life. The *jnana* of this can be attained only be *satsanga* of virtuous men who are highly proficient with *paramatha* path. *Vicara* or thoughts are awakened only be the means of *satsanga* and only by *vicara* can one free oneself from desire. It is on this path that we must resolutely march ahead.

Chapter 12

ONLY CAN THE SOUL HELP IN ITS OWN SALVATION

Lord *Srí Krsna* says in the *Srímadbhagavadgíta*- "Man should strive for the salvation of the soul by means of the soul itself. He should not let the soul be destroyed because it is the soul that is its own enemy as well as its friend. The one who gains victory over the soul with the help of soul itself, finds in the soul, a true friend. As opposed to this, the soul turns against itself if it is not won over" Here, the soul is the conscience. The conscience, being made up of the *sattvika* part of the group of *apancíkrta pancabhutan*, takes on the form of the *saksí caitanya*. The reflection of the *caitanya* is called the soul. When the reflection of the moon is seen i n a lake at night and if the water in the lake is pure and still, the moon too will appear pure and still. However, if the water is dirty and not sill, the moon too will appear to be impure and unsteady. When the reflection of teh moon appears impure and unsteady, it would be natural to attribute these qualities to the moon in the sky. Therefore, it is very important for the conscience to be pure and calm. This is only possible when the conscience does not follow the dictates of the senses and keeps the senses under control.

This subject has been explained in the *Kathopanisad* by using a chariot as a metaphor. It says that the soul is the warrior, the body is the chariot, words, touch, form, taste and smell are the roads one travels, the senses are the horses, the mind is the erin and the intellect is the charioteer. If the charioteer, which is the intellect, become highly vigilant and carefully keeps a tight control over the rein, which is the mind, all will be well.

But a little bit of carelessness and the horses, which are the senses, will throw the chariot as well as the charioteer into a ditch of destruction. On the other side of worldly pleasures lies the abode of Lord *Visnu*. The one who resists being seduced by worldly pleasures can find this abode and attain contentment. Exercising self-control helps Man to progress in every sphere of life. Only the one who takes thoughtful decisions can lead a successful everyday life. Being thoughtful enables him to say the right thing at the right time and to do things correctly.

sahasa vidadhÍta na kriyam. Do not act impulsively. The *Manasa* too says "*sahas karÍ pachitahi vimudha*" (fool who works on impulses and repents later as he does not use his discrimination) However, there are times when Man has to face situations which require making instant decisions and implementing them. Any kind of delay may cause harm. In such situations too, exercising patience and common sense are required. It is not possible for an imbalanced mind to do this. Contentment is a subtle form of patience. The contentment which enables the calm and focused conscience to support the actions of the mind, breath and senses is *sattvika* contentment. The contentment due to which the intellect is unable to relinquish fantasizing, fear, sorrow, depression and intoxication is considered to be tamas contentment. Man's personality is not built on the basis of a single incident or deed in his life but on the basis of devotion carried out over a long period of time. Just as a skilled engineer directs the flow of a river or a stream right at its inception or just as there are turns in the streets to ensure smooth flow of traffic, so does a person who is on the path of devotion to attain his highest goal, have to prepare himself beforehand. If a devotee finds his mind to be in a collected state during meditation, it should not be considered to be incidental. This state is in fact, a result of lifelong devotion. If the society at large experiences some betterment, it is because of continuous devotion to observing *dharma*, *samskrti* and *sadacara*.

It is not due to an incidental attempt on the part of just one person. The orderliness that prevailed during the rule of Lord *Rama* was not due to some miracle. It was due to devout religiousness. It is due to the absence of self-control that desire, hatred, envy, intoxication and attachment get the better of Man and lead him astray.

More than the happiness experienced through sensual pleasures is the happiness attained by restraining the senses. One who has experienced spiritual bliss will not be led astray by the false illusion created by sensual pleasures. *Nahi svatmaramam visayamrgatrsna bhramayati.* All the problems faced by Man and society today can be resolved today if one becomes introspective by means of spiritual devotion. Passively drifty with the flow of life is no characteristic of life at all. Life is about swimming against the flow and getting through it.

If only for a few moments in twenty four hours, the mind should be made steady and calm. This is possible only be the *smarana, cintana* and *dhyana* of God on a regular basis or by making a self-effort to stead the mind.

In this list our wellbeing and success. This is *paramayoga*.The result of *dana*, following one's *dharma, niyama, dama, vedadhyayana, satkarma* and *brahmacaryadi srestha vrata* is that the mind becomes focused and turns towards God.

Paro hi yogo manasah samadhih (parama yoga is when the mind of an individual is at peace, it merges with the Lord for which he has to make self-effort).

Chapter 13

KNOWLEDGE OF THE RIGHT DIRECTION IS ESSENTIAL

The highest aim of all living beings is attaining eternal bliss; however, only those who are at peace can be happy. Contentment of the mind and freedom from vices are essential for peace. Only the mind that is still and pure like placid waters can be free from passion and hatred. This is considered a truly contented individual. The person who is not easily swayed and agitated by adverse circumstances has a *susamskrta* (refined heart) which requires spiritual devotion for it to fully evolve. Some people say that the nature of the mind is such that it easily tends toward vices and, therefore, devotion is of no use. But upon reflection, we realize that devotion is stronger than nature because humankind's karma instills the samskara associated with karma into the mind. After a deed is done, time elapses and the deed no longer exists. However, the resulting samskara of the deed remains. Karmas (righteous and unrighteous) make people's minds storehouses of samskara, which eventually become their nature.

These samskara are awakened from time to time and influence the mind to perform recommended or prohibited actions in accordance to people's different emotions and thoughts. However, just as a potter can make his earthen pots only by mixing clay and water, so do the righteous and unrighteous deeds of the doer stem from their feelings of love and hatred. All action arises from the union of a cause with an aide, just as an earthen pot can be made only when clay is mixed with the aid of water. Similarly, love and hatred act as aides to each other and, together with the nature, bring about action.

Similarly, nature can do nothing without the presence of love and hatred. Therefore, even though it is difficult to restrain nature, it is possible to restrain our actions by exercising control over our feelings of love and hatred through devotion.

Wise and thoughtful people should first and foremost have a thorough understanding of their mental states through self-inquiry. By eliminating undesired emotions and adopting the desired guna, by regular self-inquiry, sadacara, satsanga, *isvararadhana*, or *atmacintana*, the mind can become strong and stable. Even in our worldly matters and associations, we must maintain peace, balance, and moderation in our hearts. We must daily (at least once a day) make our minds pure and calm. This is possible only through devotion and satsanga.

The tale of the snake and the mongoose is well known: whilst battling with the snake, the mongoose is bitten by the snake, and the poison from the bite starts spreading through the body of the mongoose. The mongoose then quickly reaches for the antidote to the poison and, after consuming it, resumes the fight and eventually defeats the snake. The world is the snake, and each devotee is the mongoose. When the poisons of the world, such as anger, passion, and desire, start affecting devotees, they should at once get rid of them through upasana, *aradhana*, or *sadhusatsanga*, and then they should resume their worldly actions after having regained their composure. In this way, in spite of being involved in worldly matters, they will be able to remain detached from them. Pure conduct also requires a pure mind. Decisions that are made by an excited mind result in chaos and regret because an unhealthy mind makes wrong decisions which result in wrong deeds. People with healthy minds are capable of avoiding wrong conduct. Our peace and happiness can be taken away from us when we let the world harm our minds, not otherwise. Gosvami Tulasidasaji says in the Vinayapatrika -*anavicara ramaniya sada samsara bhayankara bhari.sama santosa daya viveka te vyavhari sukhakari*. "The usefulness of wealth and prosperity in this world cannot be denied." But it is also a universal truth that these worldly pleasures and wealth make the mind temporarily content, but they are of no use when the mind is unhealthy or discontented. Both individuals and society require a balance between materialism and spirituality.

Today we have forgotten this fact and we are running after modernization. It is best to follow a certain direction in life, but we must also keep the goals, means, and obstacles in mind. Spiritual seekers should give serious thought to where they are heading in life. Material progress at the cost of spiritual qualities can never be beneficial to individuals or to society. This is because whatever is attained at the cost of mental peace and stability will be rendered useless due to bad intentions. Let us pray to the merciful, benevolent Almighty to help us in understanding the right direction in life and bless us with eternal peace.

Chapter 14

THE NECESSITY FOR DAILY SELF INQUIRY

The human form is God's most sophisticated creation because it is the only one endowed with the intelligence capable of experiencing the manifestation of God. The words *God*, *Brahma*, and *the Divine* are all synonymous to what philosophers call *advaya jnana-tatva*. Brahma is *sat chid ananda* (knowledge, existence, bliss). Our intense desire to attain eternal and limitless bliss becomes the cause behind all our effort. This proves that our ultimate goal is to attain sat chit and ananda.

However, this goal cannot be attained in the presence of self-conceit, a wavering mind, and a strongly desirous nature. This can only be achieved through self-inquiry, introspection, and self-control. Our daily routine and conduct should be such that it helps in our sadhana (spiritual work). The wise sages of India understood this truth through the Vedas and made it a part of their lives. Today, we are hankering after material pleasures and becoming indifferent to those spiritual values that have enabled us to control ourselves in the midst of various desires. Some people say that spiritual values help in nurturing our inner selves, which becomes an obstacle to material progress; therefore, it is preferable to neglect them. However, this is not true. In fact, the collective spirituality shown by the whole world transcends the petty self-interests of the individual and does not act as an armor to safeguard our material interests

Parama akincana priya hari kere.

This means, just as God is dear to the destitute, so are the destitute dear to God.

The sole purpose of individuals' and society's material progress is temporary happiness. The mind experiences contentment, and it is the mind rather than the physical body that associates itself with this type of happiness. When the mind is restless and discontented, these become meaningless.

We must therefore protect our spiritual values and keep them in mind as we strive for material progress.

It cannot be denied that food, clothing, shelter, and health are very important to safeguard our lives. However, materialistic achievement is not the ultimate goal in life; material things are just means for sustaining our lives. The ultimate goal is to realize God.

The discontentment and restlessness of the people from countries where material luxuries abound are an affirmation of this principle, as happiness cannot be attained through satisfying the desires but by the removal of desires.

There is a famous shloka: "*Na cendrasya sukham kincinna sukham dincinna sukham cakravartinah. sukhamasti viraktasya munerekantahivinah.*" This means, neither is Lord Indra happy, nor are the rulers of huge empires happy.

Only the secluded and detached saint is truly happy. Some people hold the view that desire is an impetus since it is desire that motivates us. Up to a certain extent this is true; however, sometimes desire pushes people toward idleness and unethical behavior. Presently, this is what we see in society.

Our scriptures consider the object that has been acquired through ethical behavior to be righteous conduct. We must work very hard and persevere to earn wealth in accordance with our religious values.

Eating pure food is of great importance for spiritual devotion:

"*Aharasuddhau satvasuddih satvasuddhau dhruvasmritih smritisuddou sarvagranthinam vipramoksah.*" This means that pure food makes the mind pure, purification of the mind causes *dhruvasmriti*, and purification of *smrti* leads to the release from all material bondage.

We cannot purify our food if we inflict pain and suffering upon others. Therefore, each person should use only that wealth which has been amassed through toil and perseverance.

In this way we can broaden the road to the collective progress of individuals as well as society by combining material progress with spirituality. In our society, only those who have combined dharma, arth, kama, and moksa are considered to be fully developed or evolved. Objects acquired in accordance to religious prescriptions should be used for religious purposes only rather than for sensual desires.

Sex is for procreation and sustaining the human species, not for sensual pleasure. The purpose of our life is tatvajijnasa (understanding its true meaning). This is our dharma (duty) which will lead to moksa (liberation).

In the present circumstances, additional efforts (purusartha) are required for the progress of individuals as well as society. Individuals and society as a whole are closely interwoven. No action of an individual should be such that it could act as obstacle to the welfare of society. In fact, our endeavors should be to develop a society (while preserving his traditional spiritual values) that provides us with unrestricted opportunities for material progress.

However, all this is not possible if we cannot keep our impulses under control. That is why it becomes necessary to make our minds patient and calm. Only those with calm and collected minds make thoughtful decisions. They are capable of leading themselves as well as society to the righteous path.

If we wish that none of our decisions or actions should cause us regret, we must resolve to always make decisions with peaceful and composed minds. At least once a day, we must make our minds calm and introspective, as a restless mind generally reacts impulsively.

With self-inquiry, separating our minds from our bodies, purification of thoughts, and meditation, our minds will gradually become placid. Peace of mind is useful not only for purification of our actions and spiritual progress, but also for our physical wellbeing.

Pratyaham pratyavekseta narascaritamatmanah.
kimaham pasubhistulyah kimva satpurusairiti.

This means that we should, on a daily basis, sit in seclusion and reflect upon whether we are passively flowing with the current of nature like an animal, or are, like the wise and virtuous people, continuously striving for a goal in spite of all obstacles. After that, we should ascertain our duties and resolutely carry them out.

We can easily attain our goals if we move in the direction as specified by the sastra and the *acarya*.

Chapter 15

THE STRENGTH OF THE MEANS OF REALIZATION LIES IN ITS PERSISTENCE

Bhagvat tatva vijnana is the means of attaining release from the threefold sufferings (*trvidha tapa*), which are bodily, those caused by fate, and those caused by contact with the external world. We are always striving to attain freedom from sorrow and for absolute eternal bliss. On reflecting upon the purpose of all the desires of humanity, we see that we have divided the world into two parts—that which is to be given up and that which is to be attained. However, we can see that we are unable to achieve our purpose by this means. We wish to avoid unhappiness and its causes—anxiety, illness, sorrow, suffering, old age, and death—however, these are inevitable. Similarly, when we are unable to fully amass happiness and the means of its enjoyment in spite of working hard, we are unable to stop them from being separated. In spite of all efforts, the dissatisfaction and yearning in our hearts remain. The cause of this dissatisfaction is not the absence of enjoyment, but the ego and a mind that delights in enjoyment of pleasures. To demonstrate a lacking in oneself is indicative of an egoistic nature. Desires will always arise in minds that delight in enjoyment of pleasures. Enjoyment in amassing means of pleasures will only feed the egotistic and pleasure-seeking mind. As a result, dissatisfaction and yearning keep on increasing.

Only when the soul is contented are we truly happy. The limited ego requires material pleasures to feel important.

Having tasted material pleasures, we find that the yearning for them increases further. This stops us from feeling complete. Only those who do not seek external pleasures can truly experience a sense of fulfilment and completeness. This is because happiness lies within us, not outside. Just as musk lies in the navel of the musk deer, but ignorance makes the animal wander from forest to forest to seek it, so does the extroverted person wander the whole world in search of happiness when actually it lies within.

A farmer had a field near the bank of a river. One day, he went to bathe in the river. As he stood on the riverbank, he saw a sparkling gem in the clear water. Seeing this, he was filled with delight. He undressed and entered the water. He kept diving in to look for the gem, but all he could find were stones and pebbles. Each time he came out of the water, he could still see the gem under the water, and he would became confused. Then he would dive in again. Coincidentally, a wise and noble man arrived on the scene. He asked the farmer to explain the cause of his confusion. Then he instructed the farmer to come out of the water and climb onto the branch of a tree to see the reflection in the water. Paying heed to the wise man's instructions, the farmer climbed the branch of the tree, and there, in a bird's nest, he found the gem he was looking for. He had simply seen its reflection in the water.

Due to the presence of favorable conditions and desired objects, the *satvaguna* in our soul is awakened, and it brings about purification and focus. As it is at this time that the soul feels happy due to the appearance of the inherent *Paramananda-svaröpa Paramatma*. However, due to our extroversion, we do not seek within ourselves; rather, we are deceived by external illusion, and we attribute happiness to this illusion. As a result, we experience distress like the farmer who kept diving into the water for the gem.

Just as a gem lying on the branch of a tree can be reflected only in clean and pure water, so is *Saccidanandasvaröpa* all-pervasive Brahma (existing at all times deep within our heart) experienced clearly only in a pure and still soul. It is concealed when the soul is restless and impure. The three gunas in our minds—satva, raja, and tama—are constantly in flux. It is only when satvaguna in the soul increases that it is made pure and still. Due to being ignorant of reality, we are motivated by desires, and we believe that the enjoyment of these pleasures brings us happiness. By making the amassing of pleasures our goal, we become absorbed in thoughts about them and efforts to achieve them.

When our minds become enlightened due to satsanga, we realize our mistake and then understand that happiness lies within us; we need not seek it outside. In reality, happiness is not created; rather, it is always lying dormant within our souls. This realization occurs due to the contentment and introspection that arises through *satvikata*. Can such a state of the soul be brought about by sensual pleasures? Never! Even if it does, it merely increases the desire for enjoyment of pleasure.

There are two kinds of people in this world. Some are absorbed in their attachment to sensual pleasures, and some are lying in wait for these pleasures. This has increased the ignorance inherent in their hearts. This is the cause of extroversion.

Extroversion can be removed through tapah and *tyaag*. The highest *tatva* is the focus of the senses and the mind.

Manasascendriyanam hyaikagryam paramam tapah.

Tyaga means to not be attracted to external illusion. Only this can lead us to *Brahmavijnana* (the true understanding of God) and *sasvatasanti* (eternal peace).

The happiness we experience when we detach ourselves from external pleasures is much greater than that which is experienced through sensual and material pleasures, which becomes stabilized by the manifestation of God (*Brahmanubhöti*)].

The devotion of devotees also makes them indifferent to external pleasures. *Manasa pöja* is of great importance in upasana.

If *bahya-pöja* qualifies as the means for total dedication, so does putting an end to amassing external pleasures qualify as tyaga. Tyaga forms the basis of devotion to the goal *tatsukhasukhitva* (to find happiness in God).

Devotees are lost in the thoughts of God (cintana) and experience rasanubhiti through *bhagavat cintana*, *bhagavatseva* and satsanga. *Moksasukha* also becomes insignificant in the face of this experience.

Na parilasanti kecidapavargamapisvara te, caranasaroja hamsakulasangavisristagrihah.

This means that renunciation of forbidden karma as per *svadharmacarana* (religious conduct), and carrying out appropriate karma results in tapah of the senses and the mind. Those who follow religious conduct experience extraordinary happiness.

In winter, we should take a dip in the Ganges in spite of the severe cold. Only those who take dips in the water, regardless of the biting cold temperature, know the joy of the experience. Likewise, religious conduct has its own unique enjoyment. Those who put in a lot of effort toward the welfare of others and lay down their lives to protect their countries will experience a kind of joy that will never be experienced by a selfish or fearful person.

Tapah and tyaga form the basis of the Indian culture. Tapah and tyaga are evident from hospitality toward guests (*atithi satkara*), dana, *paropakara*, yajna, *Devapöjana*, *Êsvararadhana*, and other such satkarma.

Self-control (*yama*) and following rules (niyama) are of utmost importance for devotion in *Astangayoga*.

Niyama is nonviolence (ahimsa), truth (satya), non-stealing (asteya), celibacy (*brahmacarya*), non-attachment to wealth (*aparigraha*), yama, purification (sauca), contentment (*santosa*), tapah, *svadhyaya*, and profound meditation on God (Êsvara-pranidhana). These are the means of self-control. Yama is even more important than niyama. These two form the basis of asana, pranayama, dharana, Dhyana, and samadhi.

We can achieve permanent bliss (*tatva darsana*) by means of any sadhana, according to our capability and interest.

What is required is a good daily regimen, faith (sraddha), willingness (*tatparata*), self-confidence (*atmavisvasa*), steady practice, and perseverance. Spiritual devotion is the right use of our time. Devotion should be observed daily, be it for just a while. *Niyama-nistha* (faith-discipline) and *nirantarata* (endlessness) brings a kind of strength to devotion by which passion and undesirable vices can be eradicated. Passion is the cause of our downfall. However, niyama is stronger than passion. Obstacles do not affect those who are strong in their devotion and observe it regularly.

Keeping our ultimate goal in mind, and thereafter continuously striving for its achievement will destroy all obstacles in the path of our spiritual progress.

Chapter 16

PURITY OF PURPOSE

According to the Srimadbhagavadgita, understanding the difference between *ksetra* and *ksetragya* is the means of achieving moksa. Desire, hatred, happiness, sorrow, breath, mind, intellect, consciousness, calmness—all are ksetra, and the soul that witnesses all these is the ksetragya. The cycle of births and deaths results from a lack of understanding of these two. Placing the happiness and sorrow of the ksetra into the ksetragya soul and considering ourselves to be happy is what makes us unhappy. This ignorance has also been considered by learned and wise philosophers to be the cause of the stirring up of emotions in the detached soul.

The purpose behind all desires of the soul is to attain total freedom from all sorrows and to attain eternal happiness. This, being the instinctive and greatest need of the human soul, is also considered to be the goal of life.

Of all life forms, only the human form is endowed with the capability to achieve this goal. Therefore, it is our highest duty to make the right use of this human life (which is difficult to attain) and perform deeds that other forms of life are incapable of performing. The human body is capable of enjoying sensual pleasures, but enjoyment of these types of pleasures cannot be the ultimate goal. This is because they cannot free us from sorrow and make us attain eternal happiness. In fact, pleasures increase sorrow. In the Kathopanisad, Naciketa says, "Sensual pleasures diminishes the acuteness of the senses and weakens the mind." Adi Sankaracarya says that pleasures are the cause of disease. The Gita, too, considers sensual pleasures to be the cause of sorrow.

Upon reflection, it will be realized that happiness lies within us, not outside. In fact, our souls are happiness.

When the mind attains the object of its desire as a result of good karma, the fulfilment of the desire brings focus and the attainment of the desired object brings joy. As a result of this, satvaguna are awakened in the soul for some time, which makes the mind calm and pure. The bliss that is experienced at that time by the soul (which is but a reflection of the ultimate bliss that lies within us) deceives us into thinking that the happiness experienced is material and sensual. However, the happiness experienced is that of the soul. It is the emotions that make the eternal and limitless mind feel as if it is lacking something. Ignorance makes the soul seek external objects to remove this feeling of lack. This takes the form of sexual desires, which give rise to other desires. As long as desires remain, the mind keeps on experiencing feelings of incompleteness and discontentment. These desires keep pricking the soul like a thorn until they are fulfilled. When the desired objects are attained, for some time there is a feeling of relief from the suffering. However, other desires are aroused again, and the suffering returns. Actually, once a desire is fulfilled, the mind returns to the same state it was in before the desire was aroused. Thus, it is confirmed that this is not the right means of attaining total freedom from sorrows and the path eternal happiness. The true means is spiritual knowledge. In the Gita, God calls spiritual knowledge to be a form of Himself.

Adhyatmavidya vidyanam.

This means that, of all the different types of knowledge, spiritual knowledge represents the true form. It is only through this knowledge that we can achieve our goals.

Our sastra speak of four types of goals: *pamara*, *visayi*, *sadhaka*, and *siddha*. Pamara are those who are ignorant of what is appropriate and inappropriate, what is religious and unreligious, and those who do whatever their minds and senses tell them to do. Visayi are those who, through the *sravana* of the sastra, have understood what is righteous and what is unrighteous. They carefully avoid the nonreligious path and agree that the righteous path is the surest means of achieving worldly happiness. Sadhaka are those whose minds have been purified through devotion to God, through carrying out desire-free karma, relinquishing the desire for enjoying all kinds of pleasures, and endlessly striving for the realization of God through *aradhana*, upasana, and *Brahmavicara*. One who has seen the manifestation of God is a liberated person (*jivanmuktamahapurusa siddha*). Siddha is the one who has accomplished the ultimate goal in life.

We should become devotees. To be devotees, it is not necessary for us to renounce domestic life (grhasthasrama). Keeping the senses and the mind under control through religion and devotion is possible even in grhasthasrama.

Lord Brahma says in the Gita that passion is a thief and the house is a prison unless we become devotees of Lord Krishna. Apart from pamar, even visayi is an inferior sadhaka. The siddha too is a lifelong devotee as he is not conceited about his siddhi.

A righteous purpose purifies all karma and emotions. By nature, no karma is superior or inferior. What is important is that it should be carried out as prescribed by the sastra with good intentions.

The superiority and inferiority of karma that are carried out in accordance to the sastra have the same basis. The question is not about who has done what; rather, the question is what was the intention behind the karma? The intentions differentiate yajna, dana, tapah, and other such good karma into satvika, rajasika, and tamasika qualities.

If we make the realization of God the goal of our lives and always keep it in mind, it is natural that our karma and emotions will become virtuous. The cause of unethical and unruly behavior in our society today is our ignorance of the true goal of our lives. Without thinking, we are blindly following others. This state is highly detrimental to individuals and to society.

We should, through satsanga and by studying the *sadgrantha*, determine our duty by keeping in mind what is appropriate and what is inappropriate.

Chapter 17

MAKE LORD RAMA YOUR IDEAL

Our behavior is intimately related to the highest and divine truth (parmartha). Only those whose behavior is pure can attain parmartha. A person's behavior reflects his or her intellectual level and the quality (guna). We cannot always depend on the intelligence of others when we face difficult situations, which abound in this world. Keeping the company of wise and intelligent people, though beneficial and of great importance, is not always possible. They are not always at our disposal or easily available. Sometimes, certain situations arise that force us to make our own decisions and act accordingly. On such occasions, it is our resourcefulness and intelligence that guides us. Only by standing atop the haven of intelligence and knowledge can we remain unaffected by the sorrows and sufferings of the world. It has been said:

Prajnaprasadamarugya asocyah socatojananbhömisthaniva sailasthah sarvan prajnonupasyati.

This means, just as a man standing on the top of a mountain peak looks down and sees people moving about and who all appear very tiny from where he is standing, so should one stand atop one's palace of wisdom and intelligence and, detaching oneself from all sorrows, should observe those who carry the weight of their sorrows and miseries around with them.

Being physically fit, having good mental health, and having a righteous moral character help in all aspects of life.

However, the importance of this can be understood only by those who have noble purpose. By having fixed goals in our lives, we can become noble and develop a strong resolve with the help of the highest means.

Yadrisaih sannivisate yadrisascopasevate.

yadrigicchecca bhavitum tadrigbhavati pörusah.

This means that we partake of the characteristics of the company we keep, of the people we serve, and those whom we wish to become like.

Just as we have to use a mirror when we endeavor to improve our appearance, so must we deeply contemplate upon the character of an ideal and noble person for the development of his inherent sadguna. The character of Lord Rama epitomizes the character of an ideal person. According to Yogavasistha, Lord Rama became an ascetic very early in life. This worried his father, King Dasaratha, who sent Yogavasistha to impart knowledge to Lord Rama. The jnana that Lord Rama acquired from Yogavasistha enlightened him. He was loved by all as the divine sadguna were awakened in him from early childhood. Maharsi Valmiki has described many of his excellent qualities. He always kept a calm mind, used gentle words, and was soft spoken. If someone spoke harshly to him, he remained silent and did not retaliate. He had a humble mind and he appreciated and never forgot even a small act of favor toward him by anyone. At the same time, he easily forgave and forgot those who had offended him. While practicing the use of weapons and learning warrior skills, he used to hold discussions in accordance to the Saastras, with wise and mature people.

He was highly intelligent, soft spoken, and always the one to initiate talks. He always put forth his refined arguments in front of assembled crowds. His words were also well meant. In spite of being extraordinarily strong, he was not proud of his strength. He was devoted to righteousness and respected the elderly. His people had great faith in him and loved him dearly. In turn, he remained a responsible and nurturing leader.

He had great compassion for the sufferings of others and had full control over anger. He was religious and worshipped brahmans. He was benevolent toward the needy, had disciplined senses and kept them under control. He was devoted to his religion and was compassionate, generous, and protective of those who sought his refuge. He considered religious conduct to be the basis of divine virtue. His mind was never inclined toward any vices, and he refused to hear any ill spoken against righteousness. During any conflict, he maintained his rationality like Vrhaspati. He was healthy, youthful, knowledgeable of the state of affairs of his country, perceptive of the sufferings of his people, and was pious. He was thoroughly learned, knowledgeable, and knew the deeper meaning of the Vedas. Lord Rama should be kept as the ideal for all spiritual aspirants. His exemplar qualities reflect the eternal peace he found within himself.

Sri Guru Gita
Achintya Vyaktarooopaya Nirgunaya Gunatmaney
Samasth jagadadharamoorthayeh brahmaney namaha

Chapter 1

Prostrations to Brahman, the unthinkable, the unmanifest, beyond the three Gunas (Sattva, Rajas & Tamas qualities of Nature) yet the Self of Gunas, the Substratum behind the whole universe.(1)

Rushya Uvacha
Suth Suth mahapragna nigama gama paraga
Guru swaroopa masmakam broohi sarva malapaham

The Sages said: O Suta, the wise one, who has acquired thorough mastery over the Nigamas & Agamas please, narrate to us the real nature or Being of the Guru, which has the power to remove all impurities. (2)

Yasya Sravana Matrena Dehi Dookhadwimuchyathe
Yena Margena Munayah Sarvajatwamprapedire
Yatpranya na panaryathi narah samsara bandhanam
Tadha Vidham Tatwam vakrutya madhuna Twaya

By hearing which, man becomes free from all pains and by treading which path the sages have attained the state of Omniscience, by attaining which man comes never again to the round of birth & death; please narrate that to us now, which is the Supreme Truth. (3, 4)

Gruhyada Gurhyatamam saram gurugita visoshathaha
Twatprasadachha Srotavya tatsarvam broohi sootha naha

O dear Suta, by your grace, we desire to hear from you the Supreme Truth & particularly the GuruGita, which is the essence of the Truth. (5)

Namami Sadgurum Shantham Pratyaksham Shivaroopinam
Shirasa Yoga pathistham mukti kamartha siddhidam !! 1
Pratah Shirasi Shuklabjo dwinetra dwibhujam gurum
Vara bhayakaram shantham smaretthanamapoorvakam !! 2

Prasannavadanaksham cha sarvadeva swaroopinam
Tatpadodakaja dhaara nipathanthi swamoordhani !!3
Thaya Samkshalayed dehe hadynanth bahirgatham malam
Tat kshana dwirajo bhootwa jayathe sphatikopam !!4
Teerthani dakshiney paade vedasthanmukha rakshithaha
Poojayedarchitham tham thu thadamidhyanapoorvakam!! 5

Ithi Dhyanam
Manasopacharaihi sreegurum poojayitwa
Lam puthi vyayatmane gandha tanmatra prakrutyananda atmane sreegurudevaya namaha
Puthi vyatmakam gandham samarpayami. Hum aakashatmane shabd tanamatra prakrutyanandatmaney sreegurudevaya namaha aakashatmakam pushpam samarpayami. Yam vasvatmaney spartinmatra prakrutyanandatmaney sri guru devaya namaha. Vasvatmakam dhoopam aadhayapayami. Ram tejatmaney roop tanmatra prakrutyanandatmaney sri guru devaya namaha. Tejatmakam deepam shiyami. Vam apatmaney rasa tanmatra prakrutyanandatmaney sri guru devaya namaha. Aapatmakam naivedhyakam nivedayami. Sam sarvothmaney bath prakrutyanandatmaney sri guru devaya namaha. Sarvatmakaan bopacharaan samarpayami.
Ithi manasapooja!

Ithi sam prathithaha sootho muni samdheirmuhurmuhuhu
Kuthoohalena mahatha provacha madhuram vachaha

Thus repeatedly prayed to by the rishis, Suta pleased by this request, spoke these divine words. (6)

Sootha Uvacha
Kshunudhavam munayaha sarvesrddhaya paraya muda
Vadami bhavarogadhni geetha matru swaroopineem

Suta said, O Rishis, hear with rapt faith & attention. I shall now narrate to you the GuruGita which destroy the cycle of rebirth & protects like a mother. (7)

Pora kailsa shikhare siddha gandharvasevithe
Tatra kalpa latha pushpa mandire athyantha sundare
Vyagrajiney samasinam shukadi munivanditham

Bodha yantham param tatwam madhye muniganam kwachith
Pranamra vadana shaswannamskurvantha madaraath
Dushtava vismayamapanna parvathi paripucchati

On the summit of Mount Kailasa, habited by Siddhas & Gandharvas, in the most beautiful temple created by Kalpa Vruksha flowers, surrounded by rishis, seated upon a tiger-skin, being prostrated by Suta & other rishis, while explaining the Supreme Truth, Parvati the consort of Shiva, seeing Him bowing to someone with great reverence, being very surprised, devotionally asked the Lord. (8, 9, 10)

Parvathi Uvacha
Om namo deva devesha parathpara jagadguro
Twa namaskurvathe bhaktya sura suranaraha sada

Parvati said, Om; salutations to Thee, O Lord of Gods, O teacher of the universe, O the higher than the highest, gods, men and demons always worship Thee with devotion. (11)

Vidhi Vishnu mahendradhyeirvandhyaha khalu sada bhavan
Namaskaropi kasmei twa namaskarashrayaha kilaha

Lord Brahma, Lord Vishnu, Indra and others prostrate to Thee always. I wish to know who will be the recipient of your prostrations. (12)

Bhagavan sarva dharmagna vrathaanaam vrathanayakam
Broohime krupaya shambho gurumaahatmyamutthamam

O Lord, O knower of all the Dharmas, O Shambhu, please narrate to me the glory of Guru, which is the best of all Vratas. (13)

Ithi samprarthithaha shaswanmahadevo maheshwaraha
Aananda bharithaha swanthe parvathimedambraveeth

Thus repeatedly prayed to by Parvati, the great Lord Maheshwara, spoke the following words with joy. (14)

Shri Mahadev Uvacha
Na vaktavyamidam devi rahasyathi rahasyakam

Na kasyapi pura proktham vyadh bhakthavyardham vadami tath

Lord Mahadev said, "O Devi, this Supreme Truth is the greatest of all the secrets that is why it isn't proper to reveal. I have never revealed it to any one before. But still I shall tell you because of your great devotion to me." (15)

Mamu roopasi devi vyamatasthakathayamithe
Lokopakarakaha prashno na kenapi kruthaha puraa

O Devi, you are my own Self in another form. Therefore I shall narrate this to you. This question of yours will benefit the whole world. No one else has put me this question. (16)

Yasya Deve para bhakti vyatha devey tatha guroh
Tasyeithey kathitha hyarthaha prakashanthey mahatmanaha

Who so ever has the Supreme Love & adoration for the Lord and as for the Lord, likewise for the Guru; to him these great matters, when they told, become clear of themselves. (17)

Yo Guroohu sa shivaha proktho yaha shivaha sa gurusmruthaha
Vikalpam yasthu kurveetha sa naro guruthalpagaha

He who is the Guru is Shiva Himself, so declare the scriptures, and the fact that Shiva is the Guru, is reminded to us in all the Smritis. He, who makes any distinction between the two, is guilty of the crime of uniting with his own Guru's wife. (18)

Vedshastrapuranani chethihaasadikani cha
Mantra yantra vidhyadini mohanocchatanadikam
Shaiva shaaktagamadini hyanye cha bahavo mathaha
Apa bhramshaha samasthanam jeevanam bhraantha chethasaam
Japasthapovratham teertha yagno daanam tadhevacha
Gurutatwam avignyaya sarvam vyartham bhavethpriyeh

The Vedas, the Shastras, Puranas, the Itihasas etc., the science of Mantras, Yantras Mohana, Uchatana etc., cults like the Shaiva, Agama, Shakta, etc., and other cults existing in the world today are merely false theories expressed in corrupted words which confuse the ignorant and deluded Jivas. Japa austerities, observances, pilgrimage sacrifice, charity - all these become a mere waste without understanding the Guru Tattva. (19, 20, 21)

Gurubudhyatmano nanyath satyam satyam varananey
Thallabhartham prayatnasthu karthavyascha maneeshbhihi

The Guru is not different from the conscious Self. Without doubt, this is the truth; therefore wise men should make an effort to seek knowledge of Atman from Him. (22)

Gudhavidhya jaganmaaya dehaschagnana asambhavaha
Vignaanam samprasadena guru shabdena kathayathey

The hidden ignorance, absence of the Knowledge of Self, the world- Maya, the body are all caused by ignorance (Ajnana). By whose grace one attains direct Knowledge of the Self- he is known by the name Guru. (23)

Dehi brahma bhavedhyasmath twatkuparthei vadai that
Sarva papa vishuddhatma shree guroh padasevanath

Out of compassion for you, I shall tell you how the embodied soul becomes Brahman, having been purified of all sins by serving the feet of the Guru. (24)

Shopanam papapankasya deepanam gnaanathejasaha
Guroh paadodakam samyak samsaranovatharakam

The water of the Guru's feet has the power to dry up the mire of one's sins, to ignite the light knowledge, and to take one smoothly across the ocean of the worldly existence. (25)

Agnanamoolaharanam janmakarma nivarakam
Gnaana vairagya sidhyarthai guru padodakam pibeth

For the purpose of acquiring Knowledge and dispassion, one should drink the water with which Guru's feet are washed, which uproots the ignorance and the bondage of actions of innumerable past lives. (26)

Swadeshikasyaiva cha namakeerthanam
Bhavedannathasya shivasya keerthanam
Swadeshikasyaiva cha namachinthanam
Bhavedannathasya shivasya nama chinthanam

The kirtan of One's Guru's name becomes the kirtan of Infinite Shiva, and the meditation of Guru's name becomes the meditation of Infinite Shiva. (27)

Kasi kshetram jahnawi charanodakam
Gururvisheshwar saakshath tarakam brahmanischayaha

The place where the Guru lives is Kashikshetra and the water with which the Guru's feet are washed in Ganga (River Ganges). The Guru is Lord Vishwanath personified and he is undoubtedly the living Brahman saviour. (28)

Guruseva gaya proktha dehaha syadakshayo vataha
Tatpadam vishnupadam syaath tatra dattamanstatam

The service of the Guru is pilgrimage Gaya, His body is the imperishable banyan tree, His feet are the feet of Lord Vishnu and the mind concentrated on His feet becomes set there. (29)

Guruvaktrey sthitham brahma prapyathey tatprasadathaha
Gurodhyonam sada kruyoth purusham swairinee yatha

Brahman resides in the mouth of the Guru i.e.; his words, and one attains Brahman by the grace of the Guru. One should meditate on His Guru at all times, just as a devoted wife thinks of her husband only. (30)

Swashramam cha swajatim cha swakeerthim pushtivardhanam
Yatatswaram parityajya gusmeva samashrayeth

Abandoning thoughts of your stage in life, your caste, your reputation and increasing your well-being and think of nothing other than the Guru. (31)

Guruvaktrey sthitha vidhya gurubhaktya cha labhyathey
Trailokyey sphuta vaktaro devashirvopithumanavaha

The Knowledge of Brahman resides in the mouth of the Guru. The disciples get it by devotion to the Guru. In the three worlds this fact is clearly enunciated by Divine Sages, the Pitris (ancestors) and learned men. (32)

Gukaraschandhakaro hi rukarastheja uchyathey

Agnana grasakam brahma gurureva na samshayaha

The syllable "Gu" is the darkness and the syllable "Ru" is said to be light. There is no doubt that the Guru is indeed the Supreme Knowledge that dispels (the darkness of) ignorance. (33)

Gukaraschandakarasthu rukarasthunnirodhakruth
Andha kara vinashitwavath gururityabhidheeyathe

"Gu" Kara means the darkness and "Ru" Kara means the remover of the darkness. On account of the power of removing darkness, the teacher is known by the significant name "Guru". (34)

Gukarascha gunathitho roopathitho rukarakaha
Gunarupaviheenatwath gururityabhidheeyathe

The letter "Gu" denotes that He is beyond the three Gunas and "Ru" denotes that He is beyond forms. Because He is free from Gunas and forms, He is called the Guru. (35)

Gukaraha prathamo varno mayadi gunabhasakaha
Rukarosthi param brahma mayabhranthivimochakam

The first syllable "Gu" represents the principles such as maya and the second syllable "Ru" the supreme knowledge that destroys the illusions of maya. (36)

Sarvasruthi shiroratna virajithpadambujam
Vidantharthapravakaram tasmatsampoojayedgurum

The holy lotus feet of the Guru shine like the two pearls (the essence) of the entire Srutis. The Guru is the exponent of the Truths of the Vedanta. Therefore one should worship the Guru. (37)

Yasya smaranamatrena gnanamutpadhathe swayam
Saha yevam sarvasampathihi tasmath sampoojayeth gurum

By the mere remembrance of whom Knowledge dawns in one automatically; he (the Guru) is one's entire wealth. Therefore one should worship the Guru. (38)

Samsaravruksha marudra pathanthi narakanovey
Yasthanuddharathey sarvan tasmai shri guravey namaha

Those who have climbed the tree of Samsara fall into the ocean of hell. Prostrations to that Guru, who emancipates all such persons. (39)

Yek yev paro bandhurvishamey samuparisthithey
Guruhu sakala dharmatma tasmai shri gurave namaha

When one is faced by adverse situations,

only Guru helps just like the closest brother. Guru is manifestation of all religious, therefore, prostrations to the Guru. (40)

Bhavaaranya pravishtasya didmohabhrantha chethasaha
Yen sandarshithaha panthaha tasmai shri gurave namaha

Salutations to SriGuru who shows the right path to one whose mind is deluded by attachment and thus confused in the forest of Samsara. *(41)*

Tapatrayagni tasana ashantha praneenaam bhuvi
Guru reva para ganga tasmai shri gurave namaha

Afflicted by the three kinds of fires, the restless creatures on earth wander aimlessly. To such people the Guru is verily the Supreme Ganga. Prostrations to such Guru. (42)

Sapthasagaraparyantham theertha snana phalam thu yath
Gurupadapayo bindoh sahasramshena tatphalam

Whatever the merit is acquired from pilgrimages and bathing in the sacred water extending to the seven seas by one, cannot be equal to one-thousandth part of the merit derived from partaking the feet-washed water of the Guru. (43)

Shive rushtey guruswatha gurou runtey na kaschan
Labdhwa kulgurum samyaggurumeva samasrayeth

If Shiva is angry, the Guru saves you; but if the Guru is angry, even Shiva cannot save you. Therefore, with every effort, take refuge in the Guru. (44)

Gukaram cha gunatheetham rukaram roopavarjitham

Gunaatheethamaroopam cha yo dadhath sa guruhu smruthaha

The syllable "Gu" is that which transcends all attributes, and the syllable "Ru" is that which is without form. The Guru is said to be the one who bestows the state that is beyond attributes (and form). (45).

Atrinetraha shivaha sakshath dwibahuscha harihi smruthaha
Yochathuvedano brahma shri guruhu kadhithaha priyeh

O dear, Guru is the Shiva without three eyes; He is the Lord Vishnu with two hands. He is again Brahma with one face. (46)

Devakinnaragandharvaha pithuyakshasthu tumburuhu
Munayopina jananthi gurusushrushano vidhim

Even the Devas, the Kinnaras, Gandharvas, Pitris Yakshas and the sages like Tumburu and others do not know the right technique of serving the Guru. (47)

Tharkikaschananda saschaiva devagnaha karmathaha priyeh
Loukikasthey na jananthi guruthatwam nirakulam

People who are well versed in Tarkashastra (Logic), in the vedic Chhanda Karmakandins (one well-versed in religious ceremonies, rites and rituals), people well versed in worldly sciences - none of them knows the pure Guru Tattva in its entirety. (48)

Yagnino pi na muktaha syuhu na mukthaha yoginasthatha
Tapasa api no mukta gurutatwatparadmukhaha

Neither those who perform great sacrifices, nor yogis, nor those who practice severe austerities are liberated if they are averse to Guru Tattva. (49)

Na muktasthu gandharvaha pitru yakshasthu charanaha
Rupayaha siddhadevadhyaaha guru seva paradh mukhaha

Those who are averse to the service of the Guru cannot be expected to be liberated from the cycle of Samsara (birth and death), may be they are Gandharvas, Pitris, Yakshas, Rishis, Siddhas or Devas. (50)

Ithi Shri skaanda uttarakhande uma maheshwara samvade shri guru geethaayaam prathamodhyayaha

Thus ends the first chapter of Sri Guru Gita, being a dialogue between Shiva and Parvati in the second section of the Skanda Purana.

Atha Dweethiyodhyaha

Brahmanandam paramsukhadam kevalam gnanamoorthim
Dwandwateetham gagana sadrusham tatwamasyadilakshyam
Yekanityam vimalamchalam sarvadheesaakshibhootham
Bhaavatheetham triguna rahitham sadgurum tham namami

Chapter -2

I prostrate myself before that Guru, the Bliss of Brahman, the bestower of Supreme Happiness, who is Knowledge absolute, transcending the pairs of opposites, expansive like the sky, the goal indicated by the great sayings like "Thou art That", the one eternal, pure, unchanging, the witness of functions of the intellect, who is above all Bhavas (mental conditions) and the three Gunas (Sattva, Rajas and Tamas). (51,52)

**Gurupadishta margena manaha shuddhim thu karayeth
Anithyam khandayetsarvam yatkimchidatma gocharam**

One should purify his mind by the method prescribed by the Guru. With the knowledge of the Self, one should reject everything else as unreal. (53)

**Kimatra bahunokthena shastrakoti shatairapi
Durlabha chitta vishranthihi vina gurukrupam paraam**

What is the use of elaborating here? Without Guru's infinite grace peace of mind is difficult even after studying millions of scriptures. (54)

**Karunakhandagapathen chitwa pashashtakam shishohu
Samyagananda janakaha sadguru sobhidheeyathey**

One who cuts as under, for the disciple, the eight kinds of attachment (doubts, pity, fear, shyness, censure, position in society, high birth and wealth), by the sword of mercy and bestows absolute Bliss is called Satguru. (55)

Yevam shrutwa mahadevi guruninda karothi yaha
Sa yathi narakan ghoran yaavacchandra divakarau

O Mahadevi, having heard the importance of the Guru, whoever indulges in vilifying the Guru goes to terrible hells and stays there as long as the sun and moon shine on the earth. (56)

Yavatkalpanthako dehastavhevi gurum smareth
Gurulop na karthavyaha swacchandoh yadi va bhaveth

One should remember his Guru as one has a body which could be till the end of the Kalpa. One should never abandon the Guru even if he becomes Self -realized. (57)

Humkarena na vakthavyam pragnashishyai kadachan
Gururagre na vaktuvyamastyam thu kadachan

Wise disciples should never speak egoistically and should never tell a lie before the Guru. (58)

Gurum twamkrutya humkrutya gurusannidhyabhashanaha
Aranye nirjale deshey sambhaved brahmarakshasaha

One who speaks to the Guru in rude or insulting manner or who wins arguments with Him is born as a demon in a jungle or in a waterless region. (59)

Advaitham bhavayennityam sarvavasthasu sarvada
Kadachidapi no kruyodadwaitham gurusannidhou

At all times and under all conditions one should feel the non duality of the Self but one should never have this feeling with his Guru. (60)

Drusya vismruthi paryantham kuryad gurupadarchanam
Thadrushasyeiva kaiwalyam na cha tadvyathirekinaha

One should worship the sacred lotus feet of the Satguru till the "seen" disappears (absence of duality). To those only there is liberation and not to those who act in contradiction. (61)

Api sampoornatatwagno gurutyagi bhavedyada
Bhavatyeva hi thasyanthakale vikshepamuthkatam

Even though one is the knower of the entire truth (knower of all shastras); if he is a Guru Tyagi (abandoner of the Guru) he will face, at the time of death, great distraction. (62)

Gurou sathi swayam devi paresham thu kadachan
Upadesham na vai kuryaath tadha chedrakshaso bhaveth

When the Guru is present one should never give teaching to others. If one does so, one becomes a demon. (63)

Na gurorashramey kuryath dushpanam parisarpanam
Deeksha vyaakhya prabhutwadi guroragna na karayeth

When the Guru is present one should not intoxicate himself or waste time in the Guru's ashram. It is prohibited to initiate disciples, give lectures, show off and order the Guru in the Guru's ashram. (64)

Nopashramam cha paryeikam na cha paada prasaranam
Naangabhogaadikam kuryaanna leelaamaparaamapi

One should not stretch legs in the front of the Guru, nor indulge in personal luxuries, nor gratify the senses. (65)

Gurooonaam sadasadwaapi yaduktam thanna langhayeth
Kurvannagna diwarathrou daasvannivased gurou

One should never ignore the words of the Guru, be it just or unjust. Carrying out his behests, one should live, day and night like a servant, with the Guru. (66)

Adatham na gurodravya muparbhujeet kahirchit
Dattam cha ramkavad graahya praanopyathena labhyathe

One should never enjoy the wealth not given by the Guru. Those which are given by Him, one should enjoy like a servant. One may thereby attain vital force. (67)

Paadukaasan shayyadi guruna yadbhishtitham
Namaskurvith tatsarvam paadaabhyaam na spusheth kwachith

Sandals, seats, beds etc; and the other articles used by the Guru should never be touched by one's feet. One should prostrate to the articles used by the Guru. (68)

Gacchathaha pushtatho guruchhaayaam na laghayeth
Nolbanam dhaarayedwesham naalamkaaram sthatholbanaan

While the Guru walks, the disciples should follow him. He should never cross the Guru's shadow. He should not wear precious dress, ornaments etc. (69)

Gurunindaakaram drushtva dhaavayedadh vaasayeth
Sthaanam vaa tatparityaajyam jihwachhedaakshamo yadi

On seeing a person speaking ill of the Guru, if one is not able to cut his tongue, one should drive out that person from that place. If the person lives there, then one should leave that place. (70)

Munibhihi pannagairvapi suraiva shaapitho yadi
Kaalamrutyu bhyaadwaapi guruhu sankrati parvathi

O Parvati, even when one is cursed by saints and gods or faced by danger from serpents, from the fear of natural death, Guru becomes the saviour. (71)

Vijaananthi mahavaakyam guroscharana sevaya
The viy sanyasinaha proktha ithare veshadhaarinaha

They who understand the meaning of the great sayings (Mahavakya) by doing service of the Guru are real Sanyasins. The others are mere wearers of the ochre-coloured dress. (72)

Nityam Brahma niraakaram nirgunam bodhayeth param
Bhaasayan bhrahmabhaavam cha deepo deepaantharam yatha

The Guru is one who instructs the disciple about attributeless, eternal Brahman, and there by reveals the Brahmanbhava (feeling of being Brahman) in his heart just like one lamp kindles another lamp is the Guru. (73).

Guru prasadathaha swatma nyatma rama nireekshanaath
Samatha mukti margena swaatma gnaanam pravarthathey

By steadiness in the path to liberation, by seeing one's own Self in oneself, by the practice of introspection within and by the Grace of the Guru, the Knowledge of the Self dawns in the Sadhaka. (74)

Sphatikey sphaatikam roopam darpena darpane yatha
Tadhatmani chidaakaaram aanandam sohamityath

Just as a crystal shines with all its beauty in a crystal, as a mirror in a mirror, so also in the Self shines the bliss of the Chidakasha "That I am" is beyond all doubts. (75)

Angushtey maatram purusham dhyaayeccha chinmayam hadi
Tatra sphurathi yo bhaavaha srunu tatkathayaamithe

Lord Shiva says to Parvati, "I shall tell you, the state of consciousness that arises in the heart when the consciousness personified Purasha of the size of the thumb is meditated in the heart." (76)

Ajo hama maroham cha hyanaadinidhanohyaham
Avikaaraschidanando hyaneeyaan mahatho mahaan

"I am unborn. I am deathless. I am beginningless. I am endless. I am changeless. I am consciousness and Bliss. I am the smallest of the small. I am the greatest of the great." (77)

Apoorvamaparam nityam swayam jyotirniraamayam
Virajam paramaakasham dhruvamaanandamavyayam

Agocharam tadhaa gamyam naamaroopa vivarjitham
Nisshabdam thu vijaaneeyaathswabhaavaad brahma parvathi

There is none prior to me and none later. I am eternal. I am self-illumined. I am disease less. I am ever pure. I am the eternal Akasha. I am without the least movement, am Bliss imperishable. (78)

O Parvati, Brahman is the unseen incomprehensible, without name and form and inexpressible by word or speech directly. This is the very nature of the Brahman. Know it thus. (79)

Yadha mandhaswabhaavatwam kapoorakusumadishu
Seethoshnaswabhaavatwam tadha brahmani shaswatham

Just as fragrance is inherent and natural camphor, flowers, etc. just as heat and cold are natural with fire and ice, so also in Brahman eternity is natural. (80)

Yadha vijaswabhavena kundala katakadayaha
Suvarnotvena tishtanthi tadhaham brahma shaswatham

Just as gold exists in its own nature in ornaments like ear-ring, bangles etc; so also I am ever permanent. (81)

Swayam tadhavidho bhootwa sthathavyayam yavakuvachit
Keeto bhrunga iva dhyaanaath yadhaa bhavathi tha ishaha

Just as a worm by the constant thought of a black bee ultimately becomes black bee itself, so also, one should by constant meditation practiced on Brahman anywhere, become Brahman. (82)

Gurodhyonirnaiva nityam dehi brahma mayobhaveth
Sthitashwa yatravatraapi mukthosou naatra samshayaha

By constant meditation on the Guru, the individual soul becomes Brahman, wherever he lives he is free, there is no doubt in it. (83)

Gnaanam vairagyamaiswaryam yashaha shri samudahatham
Shadgunau swaryayuktho hi bhagawan shri guru priye

My dear Parvati, Guru possesses the six qualities of knowledge, dispassion, lordliness, fame, wealth and sweet-eloquence. (84)

Guruhu Shivo gurudevo gururbandhuhu shareerinaam
Gururaatma gururjeevo guroranyann vidhyathey

Guru is Shiva, Guru is God. Guru is the relative of all embodied beings. Guru is the Self. Guru is Jiva. There is nothing other than the Guru. (85).

Yekaki nispruhaha shaanthaha chinthasooyadi varjithaha
Balyabhaavena yo bhaathi brahmagnaano sa uchyathey

Alone (one without a second); desire less peaceful, free from worry, jealousy etc. one who shines like a child (in his simplicity) is Brahmagnani (Knower of Brahman). (86)

Na sukham vedashaastreshu na sukham mantrayantrake
Guroh prasaadanyatra sukham naasthi maheethale

There is no happiness in Vedas and Shastras, not even in mantras and tantras. In this world, there is no happiness except in the Guru's Grace. (87)

Chaavarkavaishnavamathe sukham prabhakare na hi
Guroh paadaanthike yadvatsukham vedaantha sammatham

There is no real happiness in the philosophy of the Charvakas (which takes the body as the object of worship and say: "Eat, drink and be merry."), nor of the Vaishnavas (which preaches to worship Lord Vishnu), nor even the Prabhakaras (which in Mimansa Philosophy expounded by Kumarila Bhatta.) The happiness present in the feet of the Guru is found nowhere else. This is an admitted fact in Vedanta. (88)

Na tatsukham surendrasya na sukham chakravarthunaam
Yatsukham veetharagasya munirekanthavasinaha

The happiness that is enjoyed by a saint free from all attachments, living in seclusion, is not enjoyed even by Indra, the Lord of the Devas, or an emperor, or mighty rulers. (89)

Nityam brahmarasam peetwa thuso yaha paramatmani
Indram cha manyathe ramkam nrupaanam tatra ka katha

Having drunk Brahmarasa and satisfied in the Supreme Self, the sages of realization consider Indra also poor and then what is one to say of kings of the world? (90)

Yatha paramkaivalaym gurumarguna vaibhaveth
Gurabakthirathi karya sarvada mokshakakshibhi hi

The seekers after liberation should at all times develop Guru-Bhakti because by following the path shown by the Guru, one attains the highest emancipation. (91)

Yek yevadwetheeyoham guruvakyena nischithaha
Yevamabhyastha nityam na sevyam vai vanantharam
Abhaasannimishanaiva samaadhimadhicchhathi
Aajanma janitham paapa tatkshanadeva nashyathi

On the advice of the Guru, if one meditates with firm determination on the principle of "I am one without duality" need not resort to forest for penances, and the constant practice of the above principle brings about samadhi and his sins are burnt instantaneously. (92 & 93)

Gururvishnuhu prapya sarvasamgavivarjit
Thamaso rudraroopena sujanyavathi hanthi cha

As the Rajasic Brahma, SriGuru creates this universe, as the Sattvic Vishnu, He protects it and as the Tamasic Rudra, He destroys it. (94)

Tasyavalokanam prapya sarva samga vivarjit
Yekaki nisrpruhaha shaanthaha sthaathavyam tatprasadathaha

By His grace, after having attained a glimpse of that Supreme being in Guru, one should stay alone, free from all contacts without any attachment and peacefully. (95)

Sarvagnapadamityahrudehi sarvamayo bhuvi
Sadaananda sadaa shaantho ramathey yatra kutrachith

The jiva, which becomes omnipresent, ever-peaceful, lives happily anywhere, who is ever in Bliss is known as omniscient. (96)

Yatraiva thishtathey so pi sa desh punabhaajanaha

Muktasya lakshanam devi tavagrey kadhitham mayaa

Wherever he (the liberated soul) stays, that country accrues all merits. O Devi, I have told to you the characteristics of a liberated soul. (97)

Yadhyatyadheetha nigama shadanga aagama priye
Aadhyamadini shaastrani gnaanam nasthigurum vina

O beloved Parvati, one might have learned the four vedas and the six- branched Agamas (shiksha, kalpa, Vyakaranam, Nirukta, Astrology and Chhandas) all Adhyatma Shastras, but one cannot attain Self-knowledge without Guru. (98)

Shivapoojaratho vaapi Vishnupoojarathobhava
Gurutatwa viheenaschetatsarvam vyarthameva hi

One may be engaged in worship of either Shiva or Vishnu, but if he is without knowledge of the Guru-Tattva, all his worship is a mere waste. (99)

Sarvam syatassaphalam karma gurudeeksha prabhavath
Gurulabhatsarvalabho guruheenasthu vaalishaha

By the glory of Guru Diksha, all your actions bear fruit. By the attainment of a Guru one attains everything. One without a Guru is mere fool. (100)

Tasmatsarva prayatnena sarvasangavivarjit
Vihaya shaastrajaalan gurumeva samashrayeth

Therefore, discarding all kinds of contacts with people, by all possible means, giving up all conflicts of the scriptures; one should take refuge in the Guru. (101)

GnagnaGna
Gnana heeno gurutyajyo mithyavadi vidambakaha
Swavishranthi na jaanathi parashanthim karothi kim

The Guru devoid of Knowledge, who indulges in falsehood and who is full of vanity should be abandoned. Because when he is not able to find peace for himself, how is he to bestow peace on others? (102)

Shilaayaha kim param gnaanam shilasamdhapratharane
Swayam thanthu na jaanathi param nisathareyetkatham

What special knowledge has a stone in saving other stones from drowning? If it cannot swim across the river by itself; how can it help other stones to swim across? (103)

Na vandaneeyasthey kantha darshanath bhranthikaarakaaha
Varjayethan gurun doorey dheeraneva samasrayeth

They (such Gurus) are not at all fit to be worshipped whose reasoning creates painful delusion. Such Gurus should be abandoned from a distance. One should take refuge only in the Self-realized ones. (104)

Paakhandinaha paparatha naasthika bhedabuddhayaha
Streelampata duraachara kruthaghna bakavruthayaha
Karma bhrashtaha kshamanashtaaha nindhathakaischa vadinaha
Kaminaha krodhinaschaiva himsaaschandaaha shathasthatha
Gnaanalusa na karthavya mahapapasthatha priye
Yabhyobhinnou guruhu sevya yekabhaktya vicharya cha

O Parvati, imposters, habitual sinners, atheists, those who are of the different temperament, slaves of woman, evil-doers, ungrateful, roughish, those fallen from Karma Marga, cruel, who indulge in vain discussions, sensualists, those who are angry, violent, unyielding to reasoning, devoid of knowledge, great sinners, crooks, fools, such Gurus should be avoided; and one should only take refuge in the Self-realized Guru with single-minded devotion and discrimination. (105,106,107)

Satyasatyam puna satyam dharmasaram mayoditham
Gurugeetha samam sthotram nasthi tatwam guroh param

Whatever is declared by me in this connection is the essence of whole religion. There is no prayer equal to GuruGita there is no truth beyond Guru. It is the Truth. It is the Truth. It is nothing but the Truth. (108)

Anena yad bhavedh karyam tadvadami thava priye
Lokopakaarakam devi loukikam thu vivarjayeth

Mahadeva said- I shall tell you, O Dear Parvati, what can be achieved by the study of this GuruGita. This I narrate to you for all the benefit of the world. One should shun all worldliness from one's mind. (109)

Loukikaddhurmatho yathi gnaanaheeno bhaavaneva
Gnaanabhave cha yatsarvam karma nishkarma shamyathi

Whoever will use the Guru Gita for materialistic purposes will become ignorant and will fall into the ocean of samsara. Those who perform actions with Self-knowledge, their karmas will be nullified. (110)

Whoever will use the Guru Gita for materialistic purposes will become ignorant and will fall into the family ocean. Those who perform actions with Self-knowledge, their karmas will be nullified. (110)

Imaam thu shakti bhavena pathedwai srunuyadapi
Likhitwa yatprasadena phalamasnuthey

Whoever studies, hears or writes the GuruGita with faith and devotion attains all merits through its grace. (111)

Gurugeethamimam devi hadi nityam vibhavaya
Mahavyadhi gathaidukkhaihi sarvada prajapenmuda

O devi, one should meditate on the GuruGita in one's heart with great devotion even when one is placed with sufferings on account of incurable diseases, one should repeatedly read this with reverence. (112)

Gurugeetha ksharaikaikam mantra rajamidam priye
Anye cha vividha mantraha kalaam narhanthi shodasheem

O Devi, each & every letter and syllable of this GuruGita is a king among Mantras. Other mantras do not even deserve the credit of even one-sixteenth part of this. (113)

Anantha phala mapnothi gurugeetha japen thu
Sarvapapahara devi sarvadaridrayanashini

One acquires infinite fruits by the repetition of this GuruGita. It is the destroyer of all sins and the remover of all poverty. (114)

Akala mrutyu hantri cha sarva sankatanashini
Yaksha rakshasa bhootadi chor vyaghra vidhathini

The study of this GuruGita puts an end to untimely death and all afflictions. It also destroys the evil effects of Yakshas, Rakshasas, Bhutas (evil spirits), fear of thieves, tigers etc. (115)

Sarva pada vakunthadi dushta dosha nivarini
Yatphalam gurusannidhyath tatphalam pathanad bhaveth

The study of the GuruGita removes all afflictions, troubles, diseases like leprosy, and great sins. By the study of GuruGita one derives the benefits of the holy company of Guru. (116)

Mahavyadhihara sarvavibhoothehe siddhidaa bhavetha
Athva mohaney vashey swayameva japetsada

This Guru Gita becomes the bestower of all Siddhis (miraculous powers) and all divine Aishwaryas and remover of all kinds of diseases. In case of Mohana (to delude others) and Vashya (keeping others in submission to one's will) or to nullify the effect of Mohana and Vashya practised by others, one should always do Japa of this Gita. (117)

Mohanam sarvabhoothanam bandhamokshakaram param
Devaragna priyakaram rajanam varamanayeth

One who studies this GuruGita with faith and devotion acquires the power to attract all. It destroys all bondages and one attains the highest liberation. It makes one favourite of Indra and also brings kings under one's control. (118)

Mukhasthambhakaram chaiva gunaanam cha vivardhanam
Dushkarmanashram chaiva tatha satkarma siddhidam

Reading and study of this GuruGita stops the power of speech of one's foe. It increases one's virtues. It destroys all evil actions and bestows success in good actions. (119)

Asiddham sadhayetkaryam navagraha bhayapaham

Du swapna nashanam chaiva suswapna phaladayakam

By reading this GuruGita, one attains success in all actions including those which are considered unsuccessful. It is the remover of the fear of the evil influences of the planets. It totally destroys all evil dreams and bestows the fruit of good dreams. (120)

Moh shanthikaram chaiva bandha mokshakaram param
Swaroopa gnaana nilayam geetha shastramidam Shive

O auspicious one, this GuruGita shastra brings peace where there is delusion.It gives liberation from all bonds. It is the storehouse of Self-knowledge. (121)

Yem yem chinthayathe kaamam tham tham prapnothi nishchayam
Nithyam sowbhagyadam punyam thapatraya kulapaham

Whatever desire a man has or thinks of that he gains through this GuruGita. It bestows external good will, fortune and merits, and destroys the three kinds of pain (Adhyatmik, Adhidevic and Adhibhautic). (122)

Sarva shanthikaram nithyam thatha vandhyaa suputradam
Aavaidya vyakaram streenaam sowbhagyasya vivardhanam

This Gita bestows all peace and permanent happiness. It is the giver of a son who is obedient and well behaved to a barren woman. For the other woman whose husband is alive, this GuruGita is the giver of all fortune and the state of non-widowhood. (123)

Ayurarogyam aishwaryam putra poutra pravardhanam
Nishkaama jaapi vidhava patheynmoksha mavapnuyath

This Gita is bestower of health, long life, prosperity, increase in sons, grandsons, etc. A widow who studies this without any selfish end attains liberation. (124)

Avaidh vyayam Sakaama thu labhatey chanya janmani
Sarvadukha bhayam vighnam Nashyethapahaarakam

A widow who studies this with expectation of worldly fruits will in other births never become a widow. It destroys all her pains, fears and obstacles. (125)

Sarvapapa prashamanam dharmakamartha mokshadham
Yem yem chinthayathe kaamam tam tam prapnothi nischitham

Study of this is a destroyer of all sins. It bestows dharma (practice of religion), Artha (acquisition of wealth), Kama (fulfillment of desires) and Moksha(liberation). He certainly attains all objects of his desires. (126)

Likhithva Poojaye dhasthu moksha shriyamvapnuyaat
Gurubhaktir visheshena jaayatey hadi sarvada

Whoever writes this GuruGita and offers worship to it attains wealth and salvation. In his heart arises always particular devotion to SriGuru. (127)

Japanthi shaaktaaha souraascha gaana patyaascha vaishnavaaha
Sheivaaha paashupataaha sarvey satyam Satyam na samshayaha

GuruGita is repeated by the followers of Shakti, followers of Lord Ganpati, followers of Vishnu and followers of Lord Shiva all alike, with equal devotion. This is the Truth. This is the Truth. There is no doubt in this. (128)

Japam heenasanam kurvan heena karma phalapradam
Gurugeetaam prayaaney va sangramey ripusankatey
Japan jayam vapnothi maraney mukthidayikaa
Sarvakamaani sidhyaanthi guruputrey na samshayaha

By doing Japa without sitting on an Asana (a seat), one attains no fruit. It becomes a forbidden action. By repeating GuruGita at the time of undertaking journey, in fights, and one when faced with fear of enemies, one attains success. By doing Japa in death-bed one attains liberation. To him all acts give the desired fruits and undoubtedly so, for the son of the Guru. (129,130)

Gurumantro mukhey yasya tasya sidhayanthi naanyatha
Deekshayaa sarvakarmani sidhyanthi guruputrakey

To the person who has the Guru Mantra on his tongue, all acts become fruitful but not for others. By the power of initiation disciples attains success in all actions. (131)

Bhavamul vinaashaaya chashta pasha nivarthayeh

Gurugeetambhasi snanam thatvagna kurutey sada

Sarvashudhhah pavitrosou svabhavadhatra tishtathi
Thatra devaganaha sarvam kshetra peethey charanthi cha

For the destruction of the root of the tree of samsara and for the destruction of the eight kinds of attachments, the Knower of Truth bathes ever in the River Ganges of the GuruGita. Wherever the ever pure Guru stays in his own accord there all the gods stay. They move about the place of the residence of the Guru. (132,133)

Asanstha shayana va gachhanta sthitashtanthopi va
Ashvarudha gajarudha sushupta jagrato pi va
Shuchibhuta gyanavantho gurugeetam japanthi ye
Teshaam darshan sansparshat punarjanma na vidyate

Who are pure in heart, full of knowledge recites this GuruGita while seated, lying, moving, standing, mounted on horseback, or elephant back, waking or sleeping, - even seeing them and touching, one is liberated from rebirth. (134,135)

Kusha durvasane devi hyasane shubhrakambale
Upavishya tato devi japed ekagra manasaha

Seated on a seat of Kusha or Durva grass or a seat made of white blanket one should repeat the Japa with concentration of mind. (136)

Shuklam sarvatra vei proktam vashye raktasanam priye
Padmaasane japennityam shanty vashyakaram param

A white seat is recommended for all purpose in general. Red coloured asana is used for Vashya. One should sit in lotus posture and do Japa for Vashya or acquiring Supreme peace. (137)

Vastrasaney cha daridrayam paashaane rog sambhavaha
Medinyam Dukhamapnothi kaashtey bhavathi nishphalam

(Repeating the GuruGita) on a seat of cloth brings poverty, on stone it brings disease, on the earth it brings unhappiness, and on wood it becomes fruitless. (138)

Krishnajine Gyansiddhah mokshashri vyaghra charmani
Kushasne gyansiddhihi sarvasiddhistu kimbaley

If seated on black-deer-skin one attains Jnana, and if seated on Kusha grass seat one gets Knowledge of the Self, and if seated on woolen seat one acquires all miraculous powers. (139)

Aagnesyam Karshanam chaiva vayavyaam shatrunashanam
Nairrutyam darshanam chaiva eeshaanyaam gyanameva cha

By doing Japa facing south-east one gets the power to attract others, facing north-west one's enemies are destroyed, facing south-west one will have vision (of God) and facing north-east one will attain Knowledge. (140)

Udam mukhaha shanty jaapye vashyey poorvamukha tatha
Yaamye tu maaranam proktam paschime cha dhanaagamaha

Facing north during Japa one becomes peaceful, facing east one succeeds in Vashya, facing south one succeeds in Marana and facing west one acquires plenty of wealth. (141)

Thus ends the second chapter of Shri Guru Gita being a dialogue between Shiva and Parvati in the second section of the Skanda Purana.

Ithi shri Skandottarkhande Umamaheshvarsamvade shri Gurugitaayaam Dvitiyodhyayaha

Atha Thrutheeypdhyayaha
Atha kaamya japasthaanam kathayami varaananey
Saagarantey sarittire tirthe hariharaalaye
Shaktidevaalaye goshthe sarvadevaalaye shubhe
Vatasya dhatrya mooley va matthey vridaavane tatha
Pavitre nirmaley deshey nityanushtano pi va
Nirvedanena maunen japametat samaarabhet

Chapter -3

O Devi, now I shall describe the places where to chant the verses of GuruGita for the fulfillment of desires; on the seashores, on a river bank, or in a temple of Vishnu or Shiva; in a shrine of

Shakti, in a cowshed, in all holy temples of gods, in an ashram, under a banyan tree or a Dhatri tree; or in a Thicket of Tulsi plants. One should repeat it in silence and with detachment in a clean and pure place, whether one recites it daily or for a certain number of times. (142,143,144)

Jaapyena jayamaapnoti japasiddhim phalam tatha
Heenakarma tyajetsarvam garhitasthanmev cha

By doing this Japa, one attains success and Japasiddhi. One should abandon all forbidden acts and also renounce forbidden places, while doing Japa-Anushthan. (145)

Smashaane bilvamoole va vatmoolaantike tatha
Siddhayanti kaanake moole chootvrikshasya sannidhau

One should do the Japa in cremation grounds, under a Bilva tree or a Banyan tree, or a Kanaka tree, or a Mango tree for quicker attainment of success. (146)

Akalpa janmakoteenaam yagna vrata tapaha kriyaaha
Taaha sarvaaha saphala devi gurusantosh matrataha

O Devi, by the mere satisfaction of the Guru, all sacrifices, austerities, penances, and rites practiced in crores of births, in crores of Kalpas (world cycles), become fruitful. (147)

Manda bhaagya hyashaktascha yeh janaa naanumanvate
Gurusevaasu vimukhaaha pachyante narake shuchau

The unfortunate, the weak, those who have turned their faces against the service of the Guru, who do not believe in this teaching, suffer in terrible hells. (148)

Vidya dhanam balam chaiv tesham bhaagyam nirarthakam
Yeshaam gurukrupa naasti adho gachchanti Parvati

O Parvati, learning, wealth, strength, good fortune, all of these are of no use if one does not have the grace of the Guru. One falls down. (149)

Dhanyaa maata pitha dhanyo gotram dhanyam kKulodhbhavaha
Dhanyaa cha vasudha devi yatra syad gurubhaktata

One who has Guru Bhakti, blessed is his father, blessed is his mother, blessed is his family, and clan, blessed is the earth. (150)

Sharirmindriyam pranachcharthaha svajan bandhutaam
Maatrukulam pitrukulam gurureva na samshayaha

The body, the senses, the mother's clan, the father's clan, - all those are present in one's guru. There is not the least doubt about this. (151)

Gururdevo gururdharmo gurauv nishta param tapaha
Guroh partaram naasti trivaaram kathayami te

Guru is God. Guru is religion. The greatest penance is unshakable faith in God. I repeat this thrice with force that there is nothing greater than the Guru. (152)

Samudre vai tatha toyam ksheere ksheeram ghrute ghrutam
Bhinne kumbhe yatha kaasham tathatma paramathmani

The Jivatma (individual being) and the Paramatma (Supreme Self) are one and inseparable just as the water and the ocean, the milk and the milk, the ghee and the ghee or pot ether and Mahakasha (wide ether). (153)

Tathaiva gyanvaan jeeva paramathmani sarvada
Aikyena ramate gynani yatra kutra divaanisham

In the very same way, the realized soul is merged in the highest Self, day and night, wherever he is. The realized beings delight in this identity (with Supreme Being). (154)

Gurusantoshnadeva muktoh bhavati Parvati
Animaadishu bhoktrutvam krupaya devi jaayate

O Parvati, one becomes free from the cycle of birth and death by pleasing the Guru. By His grace, one becomes entitled to enjoy the eight Siddhis (miraculous powers) i.e. Anima, Mahima etc. (155)

Samyen ramate gyani diva va yadi va nishi
Evam vidhau mahaamouni trailokya samataam vrajet

Gurubhavaha param teertha manya teertham nirarthakam
Sarvateertha mayam devi shriguroshcharnambujam

GuruBhakti is the greatest kind of pilgrimage. Others are worthless. All places of pilgrimage are present, O Devi, at the sacred holy feet of the Guru. (157)

Kanyaabhogaratamandaaha swakantayaha paradmukhaaha
Atah param maya devi kathitanna mama priye

O Devi, I am giving out these great truths to you, not for those fools who are averse to their legally wedded wives, and indulge in enjoying other women. (158)

Abhakte vamchake dhoorte paakhande naastikaadishu
Manasaa pi na vaktavya gurugeeta kadaachan

To the devotion less, to the cheater, to the wicked, faithless, atheists, and others of their type, this Guru Gita should never be told, nor should one think of doing so. (159)

Guravo bahavaha santi shishyavittapahaarrkaaha
Tamekam durlabham manye shishyahyattapahaarkam

There are ever so many Gurus in the world who rob the wealth of their disciples. But I consider that Guru a rare one among Gurus who removes the afflictions of the disciple's heart. (160)

Chaturyavaanviveki cha adhyatma gyanavan shuchihi
Maanasam nirmalam yasya gurutvam tasya shobhate

He who is the clever, the discriminative, the knower of the truths of spiritual sciences, the pure, is really the Guru. His Gurutva (state of a Guru) shines. (161)

Guravo nirmalaah shantaah sadhavo mita bhashinaha
Kaama krodha vinirmuktaah sadachaaraa jeetendriyaaha

Gurus are those who are pure at heart, calm, collected, of a saintly nature, who speaks measured words, who are free from lust, greed etc. who have conquered their senses and who are established in good conduct (Sadacharas). (162)

Soochkadi prabhedena guravo bahudha smrutaaha
svayam samayak pareekshyath tatvanishtham bhajetsudheehi

Gurus are of many types with different capacities. They are known by names, Suchaka etc. The intelligent one should know and test for himself and seek refuge in the one who is established in Self-Knowledge. (163)

Varnajalamidam tadvad baahyashastram tu laukikam
Yasmin devi samabhyastam sa guruhu soochakaha smrutaha

The "Suchaka" Guru is one who is well-versed in letters and all external worldly sciences. (164)

Varnashramochitam vidhaam dharma dharma vidhayineem
Pravaktaaram gurum viddhi vachkastvati Parvati

O Parvati, know the instructor of the duties of the different castes and orders (Varna and Ashram), Dharma, Adharma, etc. to be of the "Vachaka" type. (165)

Panchaksharyadi mantranaam upadeshta ta Parvati
Sa Gururbodhako bhooyad ubhayormuttamaha

The Guru who initiates the disciple into the five lettered mantra etc., O Parvati, he is of the "Bodhaka" type and he is superior to the Vachaka and Suchaka types named above. (166)

Mohamaarnavasyaadi tuchchamantropa darshinam
Nishiddha gururityaahu panditastatvadarshinaha

The Guru who initiates one into the lower types of Vidyas, like Mohana, Marana, Vashya etc. is called by the name of Nishiddha Guru (Lit. prohibited Guru). (167)

Anityamiti nirdishya samsare samkataalayam
Vairaagya pathadarshi ya sa gururvihitaha priye

"The Samsara is transitory and an abode of calamities"- Viewing thus the world which is an abode of miseries, this Guru shows the path leading to Vairagya (dispassion), is known as the Vihita Guru. (168)

Tatwa masyadi vaakyaanaam upadeshta Parvathi
Kaaranaakhyom guruhu proktho bhavaroga nivarakaha

The Guru who initiates the disciple into Mahavakya, Tattvamasi (Thou are that) etc. O Parvati, he is called the Karanakhya Guru. He is the remover of the disease of this mundane world. (169)

Sarva sandeha sandoha nirmoolan vichakshanaha
Janma mrutyu bhayagno yaha sa guru paramo mathaha

He, who is expert in total removal of all types of doubts, and who removes the fear of birth and death, is considered to be the "Parama Guru". (The Supreme Guru) (170)

Bahujanma kruthat punyallabhyathey sou mahaguruhu
Labdhwa mun punaryathi shishya samsar bandhanam

One gets such a Supreme Guru as a result of merits acquired in many births. Having attained such a Guru, the disciple never falls prey to bonds to Samsara, he is liberated forever. (171)

Yevam bahuvidhalokey guravaha santhi Parvathi
Theshu sarva pratrena sevyom hi paramo guruhu

O Parvati, there are in the world thus many kinds of Gurus, of all these, one should by all means and efforts, serve the Param Guru. (172)

Parvathi Uvacha
Swayam moodha mrutyu bheethaha sukruthadwirathim gathaaha
Daiwannishiddha guruga yadi tesham thu ka gathihi

Parvati said, "I want to ask you the fate of those who by chance approach and serve a Nishiddha Guru. They are themselves deluded. They are afraid of death and indifferent to good deeds."(173)

Shree Mahadev Uvacha
Nishiddha gurushishyasthu dushta sankalpadooshithaha
Brahma Phalayaparyantham na punaryati mrutyuthaam

Mahadev said, the disciple of a Nishiddha Guru, impelled by evil and wicked desires of a harmful nature, never again gets a human body until the close of Brahma Pralaya which takeplace after hundred thousand of divine years. (174)

Shrunu tatvamadim devi yada syadwirathonaraha
Tadaa savadhikaareethi prochyathey sruthamastakaihi

O Devi, hear the truth when one is endowed with dispassion, the srutis say that he is a properly qualified student. (175)

Akhandai karasam brahma nityamruktam niraamayam
Swasmin samdarshitham yena sa bhavedasya deshikaha

One who enables the aspirant to see within himself the one indivisible, homogenous Brahman, which is ever free, free from pain, immortal, should be the Guru. (176)

Jalanam saagaro raja yatha bhavathi Parvathi

Gurunaam Tatra sarvesham rajayam paramoguruhu

Just as the ocean is the king of waters, the Param Guru is the King among Gurus. (177)

Mohadirahithaha Shaantho Nityatuso nirasrayaha
Thuneekrutha Brahma Vishnu Vaibhavaha paramo guruhu

A Param Guru is free from attachment, etc; peaceful, always contented in Himself, independent, and one who considers the status of Brahma and Vishnu like a blade of grass. (178)

Sarvakala Videseshu Swatantro nischalssukheehi
Akhandai karasa swadathuso hi paramo guruhu

One who is independent at all times and places, who possess an unshakable mind and always blissful, who experiences the homogenous essence of the Self, such a one is the Param Guru. (179)

Dwaitha dwaitho vinirmukthaha swanubhooti prakashavan
Agnaana andhamashchetta sarvagna paramo guruhu

One who is free from the feeling of duality and non-duality, who shines by the light of His self-realization, who is able to destroy the deep darkness of ignorance, and is omniscient, He is a Param Guru. (180)

Yasya darshan matrena manasaha syath prasannatha
Swayam bhooyath dhruthishhanthihi sa bhaveth paramo guruhu

By whose mere Darshan (look with devotion), one attains calmness, cheerfulness, and peace and steadfastness, and peace of mind, such a one is Param Guru. (181)

Swashareeram shavam pashyan tatha swathmaan madvayam
Yaha stree kanaka mohaghna sa bhaveth paramo guruhu

One who looks upon his own body as a corpse, and his Self as the non-dual Brahman, and who has killed the infatuation for wealth and women, such a person is a Param Guru. (182)

Mouni vagmeeth tatvagno dwidhabhoochhrunu Parvathi
Na kashwinmounina labho lokey sminbhavathi priyeh
Vagmi thootkatasamsara sagarottharana kshamaha
Yatho sou samshayacchettha shastra yuktha anubhoothibhihi

O dear Parvati, listen to me. There are two classes of knowers of Truth. They are (1) The Mauni, and (2) The Vakta. No benefit accrues from the Mauni to any person. (183)

The Vakta on the other hand, is capable of saving others from great whirlpool of Samsara. Because he is able to clear all doubts by his knowledge of the scriptures, logical and convincing arguments and by his own direct Self-realization experience. (184)

Gurunama Japodhevi bahujanmarjithanyapi
Papani vilayam yanthi nasthi sandeyhamanvapi

By the Japa of the Guru's name, O Devi, the sins accumulated in the countless lives are destroyed. There is not the least doubt about this. (185)

Kulam dhanam balam bandhavassodara imey
Marano nopayujjyanthey gurureki h tharakaha

Family traditions, wealth, strength, shastras, relatives, brothers, - none of these are useful to you at the time of death. Satguru is the only saviour. (186)

Kulameva pavitram syath satyam swagurusevaya
Thasaha syassukalaha deva brahmaa-dha gurutarpanaath

By the service of the Guru, truly the entire family is purified. By the satisfaction of the Guru, all the devas, Brahma, etc. become satisfied. (187)

Swaroopa gnan shoonyena kruthamapyakrutham bhaveth
Tapo japadikam devi sakalam balajalpavath

Without the Knowledge of the Self whatever Sadhana is done is fruitless. O Devi, penances, japas, etc., everything becomes like the prattling of a child. (188)

Na jananthi param tatwam gurudeekshaparadmukhaha
Bhavanthaha pashusama hyethey swaparignanavarjithaha

Those who are averse to Guru Diksha (initiation) will never know the Supreme Truth. Without this knowledge, they are like animals. (189)

Tasmatkaivalya sidhyardham gurumeva bhajethpriyeh
Gurum vina na jananthi moodhas tatparam padam

For the attainment of emancipation from the cycle of birth and death, one should propitiate one's Guru, O dear Parvati, without a Guru, the deluded ones of the world cannot know the Supreme Truth. (190)

Bhidhyathey hruday granthischidhanthey sarva samshayaha
Ksheeyanthey sarva karmani guro karunaya Shivey

All knots of the heart are rent as under, all doubts are cleared, all the karmas are destroyed by the grace and mercy of the Guru, O Parvati. (191)

Krutaya gurubhakthesthu videsastranusarathaha
Muchyathey paathkaad ghorodh gurubhakto viseshataha

A Guru-Bhakta (one devoted to the Guru) becomes free from all capital sins, by the practice of devotion to the Guru according to the injunctions of the scriptures. (192)

Dussangam cha parityajya papakarma parityejeth
Chitta chihwa midam sasya tasya deeksha vidheeyathe

One who has abandoned the company of sinners and sinful acts, whose heart is free from sins, to him is Guru Diksha ordained. (193)

Chittatyaga neeyuktashva krodha garva vivarjith
Dwaith bhav parityagi tasya deeksha vidheeyathey

One whose heart is fixed in renunciation, who is free from anger and pride, who has abandoned the feelings of duality, to such a one Diksha is ordained. (194)

Yethallakshanasamyuktham sarvabhoothhith ratham
Nirmalam jeevitham yasya thasya deeksha vidheeyathe

One whose life is endowed with these characteristics, who is interested in the welfare of all beings of the world, whose life is pure and untained, to him is Diksha ordained. (195)

Atyantha chittapakwasya shraddha bhaktiyutasya cha
Pravaktatyamidam devi mamatma preethaye sada

O Parvati, this truth should be revealed to one who is endowed with intense devotion and faith towards the Guru, whose heart is pure to the greatest degree. It gives me the greatest satisfaction and joy. (196)

Satkarma paripakaachha chitthashuddvisya dheemathaha
Sadhakasyeiva vakthavya gurugeetha prayatrathaha

To the intelligent one possessing purity of heart, to one in whom good actions are fructifying, only to that qualified Sadhaka this Guru Gita should be imparted, even with great effort. (197)

Nasthikaya kruthaghnaya daambhikaya shathaaya cha
Abhaktaaya vibhaktaaya na vachheyam kadachan

To the atheist, to one who does evil to one's well-wisher, the hypocrite, a non-devotee, to one opposed to the Guru- this Guru Gita should never be told. (198)

Streelolupaaya moorkhaya kamopahathchethase
Nindakaya na vaktavya gurugeetha swabhavathaha

To the sensualist who carves ladies' company, the fool, whose mind is conquered by lust, desires, etc. to one who usually speaks ill, this Guru Gita should never be told. (199)

Yekakshar pradatharam yo gurunaiva manyathe
Shvanayonishatham gatwa chaandaleshvapi jaayathe

He who does not respect and honor the Guru, such a man takes innumerable births in wombs like that of a dog, and ultimately takes birth in the womb of a Chandala. (200)

Gurutyagaad bhavenmrutyurmantra tyagaadharidrath
Gurumantra parityagi rouravam narakam vrajeth

By abandoning one's Guru, one goes to death, by renouncing the Guru mantra, one endures poverty. The abandoner of the Guru and Mantra go to the hell known as Raurava. (201)

Shivakrodhad gurustratha gurukrodhacchivo na hi
Tasmatsarvprayatnena guroragnam na langhayeth

The Guru is able to save one from the anger of Shiva. But not even Shiva can save if one incurs the Guru's anger. Therefore, one should by all means and efforts take care that one does not disobey the Guru's orders. (202)

Sasakoti mahamantra shvitta vibhavamshakarakaaha
Yeka yeva mahamantro guru rityakshardwayam

The seven million Mahamantras cause more restlessness of the mind. There is only one Mahamantra comprising of the syllables "Gu" and "Ru". (203)

Na mrusha syadiyam devi madrukthihi satyaroopini
Gurugeethasamam stotram nasthi nasthi maheethaley

O Devi, my declaration shall never become untrue. Whatever is said by me is the very form of the truth. There is no stotra equal to the Guru Gita in the whole world. (204)

**Gurugeethamimaam devi bhavadookha vinaashineem
Gurudeeksha viheenasya puratho na pathekthvachith**

The Guru Gita is the dispeller of the pains of Samsara. O Devi, this should never be read out to one who has not got Guru Diksha (initiation from the Guru). (205)

**Rahasyam atyantha rahasyamethanna papina labhamidam maheswari
Aneka janmarjita punyapakad gurosthu tatwam labhathey manushyaha**

O Maheshwari, this is the secret of all secrets. It should not be imparted to a sinner. It is only by the virtuous deeds done in innumerable births fructifying in a person that he becomes eligible to get this great truth. (206)

**Sarvateertha vagahasya samprapnothi phalam naraha
Guroh padodakam peethva sesham shirasi dhaarayan**

By drinking the water after washing the holy feet of the Guru and sprinkling the remains on the head, one attains the fruit of bathing in all sacred rivers and of all pilgrimages. (207)

**Guru upadodakam panam guror ucchishna bhojanam
Gururmoorthey sada dhyaanam guronormanaha sada japaha**

One should always drink the Guru's feet washed water, eat the remnants of His food, meditate on His form and repeat His name. (208)

**Gurureko jagatsarvam Brahma Vishnu Shivatmakam
Guroh paratharam nasthi tasmat sampoojayed gurum**

The entire creation consisting of Brahma, Vishnu, and Shiva is all Guru only. There is nothing greater than the Guru. Therefore one should worship the Guru. (209)

**Gnaanam vina mukti padam labhyathey gurubhaktitaha
Guroh samanatho nanyath sadhanam gurumarginaam**

By the devotion practiced towards the Guru, one attains the liberation even without knowledge. For those who practice unflinching devotion to the Guru, no other sadhana is required. (210)

Guroh krupa prasadena Brahma Vishnu Shivadayaha
Samathyarma bhajan sarve srushti sthithyanthakarmani

It is by the Guru's grace and blessings that Brahma, Vishnu and Shiva become capable of performing their respective duties- creation, preservation, and dissolution. (211)

Mantra rajamidam devi gururityakshara dwayam
Smruthiveda puranaanam sarameva na samshayaha

O Devi, the two-lettered word "Guru" is the king among all mantras. It is the essence of the Vedas, Smritis and Puranas. (212)

Yasya Prasada dahameva sarvam mayyeva sarvam parikalpitham cha
Ithham vijanami sadatma roopam tasyam ghripaghnam pranathismi nityam

By whose grace that one realizes "I am everything, everything is superimposed in me, I offer my salutations and worship to my self-realised Satguru's lotus feet. (213)

Agnanathimirandhasya vishaya kranthchethasaha
Gnana prabha pradanena prasaadam kuru me prabho

O Lord, by the gift of the light of knowledge, may Thy blessings be bestowed on me, whose eyes are covered by the cataracts of ignorance, and whose mind is captured by sense pleasure. (214)

Ithi Shree Skanda uttarakande Uma Maheshwara Samvade Shree gurugeethayam truteeyodhyayaha

Thus ends the third chapter of Guru Gita being a dialogue between Shiva and Parvati in the second section of the Skanda Purana.

Glossary

A

Asana - yoga posture

Atmavisvasa - self-confidence

Abhaya - fearlessness

Advaya jáanatatva - Advait tatva

Ahimsa - nonviolence

Aparigraha - non-covetousness

Aradhana - worship

Artha - wealth

Astanga yoga - eight-fold path of yoga

Asteya; non stealing

Atithi satkara - hospitality

Atma cintana - self contemplation

Atma niriksana - self enquiry

B

Bhava suddhi - purification of emotions

Bhagavat tatva vijáana - realization of the Lord

Bhagvat cintana - meditation on the Lord

Bhagavad bhajana - worship to the lord

Bhagavad dharma - haven of Godliness

Bhagvat prapti - attainment of the Lord

Bhagvat seva - service to the Lord Brahma anubhuti - realize the supreme

Brahmacarya - first stage of the human life when a person is a student

Brahman - the supreme

Brahmavicara - listen, reflect, and meditate on the Lord.

Brahmavidya - supreme knowledge

Brahmavijáana - kowledge of the supreme

Brahmina -

Buddhi - intellect

C

Citta suddhi - soul purification

D

Dana - charity

Devapujana - worship of the Lord

Devarisi Nsrada - celestial sage

Dharana - concentration

Dharma - righteousness

Dharmartha- for religion

Dhçti - calmness

Dhruvasmçti - strong memory

Dhyana - meditation

Draupadi - daughter of King Draupada, married to the five Pandava brothers and thus had five husbands

Durguna - vices

G

Ghora - extreme

Gosvami Tulasidasa - (who was he and what his role was)

Grahasastrama - the second stage in the life of a person in which he leads a family life

Guna- quality

I

Êsvara aradhana- worship of the Lord Êsvara pranidhana- surrender to the Lord

J

Japa - repitition of prayers Jivanmuktamahapurusa- a person who is liberated in his living time

Jnana - wisdom

Jáanendriya - sense organs

Jáanavçdhhi - increasing wisdom

K

Kama - desire or lust

Karma - action

Karpanya dosa - the four sects of the caste system: Brahmin, Kshatriya, Vashya, Shudra

Karta - the doer

Kçyasuddhi - purification of actions

Ksatriya dharma – *kshatriya* means warrior, and his duty in life is to fight for righteousness and to safeguard it at all costs

Ksetra - body

Ksetragya - knower of the body

M

Moksa - liberation

Moksasastra- Vedanta

Moksa sukha- bliss

Mudha- fool

N

Nirantarata - continuity

Niyama - one of the Astanga yoga

Nistha- belief

P

Pamara - stone

Paramananda - svarupa-paramatma - form of the self

Paramartha - for the sake

Paramparagat a - desires that have carried on from aeons

Paropakara - good deeds

Pranayama - control of the breath

R

Rajasa - action

Rajasika (rajas) - movement

Rasanubhuti - the experience of an emotion in the mind

S

Saccidanandasvarupa - Another name of the Supreme Lord

Sadacara - right conduct

Sadgrantha - scriptures

Sadguna - virtues

Sadhaka – spiritual aspirant

Sadhu satsanga - in the company of sages

Sadicca - good desires

Samadhi- profound meditation

Samsara - cycle of birth and death

Samskara - inherent qualities, an inborn power or faculty, instinct

Santosa - contentment

Sannyasi - monk or renunciate

Sarvabhutagruhasaya - one who resides deep
    in the heart of men

Sat cit ananda - Satkarma -

Satkarma - good deed

Satpurusa - virtuous man

satsanga - the company of sages

Satvaguna - puri ty

Satvika (satva) - the quality of purity

Satya - truth

Sasvatasanti - eternal truth

Santi - peace

Sastra - a work or book dealing with religion

Sauca - purification

Sravana - hearing

Siddha - evident

Sukha - happiness

Susamskçta - person who is gifted with all the
    good inherent qualities.

Svadharma acarana - working righteously

Svadhyaya- learning by oneself

T

Tamasika (tamas) - lethargy

Tapa - penance

Tatparata - readiness

Tatva - supreme spirit

Tatvajinasa - desire to k now the essence of
    human soul

Tatvajnana - knowledge of the real nature of
    entities

Trividha tapa - the three miseries in life
    (nature, physical, and spiritual)

Tyaga - sacrifice

U

Upasana - worship

V

Vicara suddhi - purification of thoughts

Vipramoksa - liberation

Visayi - endowed with all his attachments

Y

Yajáa - sacrifice

Yama - Lord of Death,

Yogabhakti - path of devotio

About the author

Manjula rao is a spiritual person and from a very young age she pursued the path of spiritual truth culminating in higher studies of the philosophy of Adi Shankaracharya from Mumbai University.She had the divine fortune of being accepted as the disciple of His Holiness Shankaracharya Swami Swaroopanand Sarasvati. Impressed by her dedication on the spiritual path and permitted her to bring his teachings to the outside world.

Printed in the United States
By Bookmasters